PRAISE FOR *THE DATA DRIVEN LEADER*

"We need to think differently about the role of HR in business, and effectively using data and analytics to drive your business and talent strategies is now an imperative. If you're trying to understand how you can use data and insights about your talent for real business results, this is the book to read. *The Data-Driven Leader* describes practical ways you can use data to talk about your company's most valuable assets— your people."

—Kelly Palmer, Chief Learning & Talent Officer, Degreed

"The most effective leaders today are leveraging the incredible power of People Analytics to maximize talent in the organization. *The Data Driven Leader* is a practical guide for business leaders and human capital professionals to immediately make an impact with analytics. Dearborn and Swanson not only showcase where People Analytics can make the greatest difference, they include graphs, charts, checklists and step-by-step examples which can be put to use immediately. This is a must have resource for any leader of people."

—Kevin Oakes, CEO, Institute of Corporate Productivity

"Dearborn and Swanson are keenly tuned into the traditional/ stereotypical HR mindset and equally insightful about the data-based transformation needed to make more effective decisions and high-performing organizations. Data driven leaders of all functions experience greater cross-functional success when they begin with facts and master the art of drawing meaning from those facts. Every aspect of the internal and external customer experience will benefit from using data analysis to prioritize the 'why' above the 'blame' when solving problems."

—Carol Goode, SVP & CHRO at Brocade

"*The Data Driven Leader* offers an engaging parable that brings to life the value of analytically-based people decisions, and helpful guidance for leaders to enhance those decisions."

—Dr. John W. Bourdreu, professor and research director, Center for Effective Organizations and Marshall School of Business, University of Southern California

"*The Data Driven Leader* is a terrific call to action for HR leaders who want—and need—to be business leaders. Jenny Dearborn and David Swanson offer a thoughtful argument for why complex business and people challenges demand analytics-based solutions, and more importantly, they provide practical tools to make it happen. The future of work and HR is becoming increasingly analytics-based and multi-disciplinary in nature, with a value chain that is morphing from big data to better insights to business outcomes."

—Ian Ziskin, president, Exec Excel Group LLC and former chief HR officer, Northrop Grumman and Qwest Communications

"Jenny and David bring to light the best practices for leveraging data to drive critical talent decisions within an organization. The concept of designing a data-driven people strategy is spot on. Human Resources teams are now on the hook for driving measurable business outcomes. This book provides the blueprint—a must read for any HR leader."

—Michael Rochelle, chief strategy officer and principal HCM analyst, Brandon Hall Group

"I love the story-telling approach to analytical lessons that Jenny and David offer. Their knowledge of (and commitment to) people, systems and data converge here in a must-read book for anyone interested in the future of HR and Leadership. Even the non-numbers oriented, like me."

—Bill John, president & CEO, Odyssey Teams, Inc.

"Effective leaders care about truth: the organizations that they really have, not the ones they think (or wish) they have. Moving a company forward requires patient and accurate insights into what people are really doing. This valuable book provides practical and clever tools for this analytical work, demystifying the application of data analytics to HR processes that serve the entire company."

—Dr. Charles Galunic, Aviva chaired professor of Leadership, professor of Organization Behavior, INSEAD Business School, FRANCE

"We live in a world where data overload and data integrity is questioned every day. Rather than running away from it, we need to boldly step up. Consequently, the ability to synthesize information, analyze data and offer compelling insights and recommendations is one of the most critical skills required by the workforce of today. The HR function has the opportunity to lead and make a huge difference in this space. *The Data Driven Leader* is an easy-to-read, insightful book that provides great ideas for practical application across many parts of a business."

—Karen Gaydon, SVP, CHRO and Corporate Marketing, Synaptics

"HR teams have a unique opportunity to transform how work is done through analytics, helping teams be more engaged and productive. *The Data Driven Leader* provides the real-life examples and practical tips you need to begin applying HR analytics that drive better people and business results."

—Robert J. Milnor, head of Planning Analytics and Reporting, Corporate Organizational Capability, Chevron

"One of the key questions for the future is the impact of artificial intelligence on human work. Here's a great contribution to that debate. Jenny Dearborn and David Swanson, through engaging examples and in-depth analyses, show how data analytics can properly empower the workforce for the future."

—Chris Anderson, head of TED

"You can't build an organization where people want to show up if you don't truly know your people and you can't truly know your people if you don't have a people analytics strategy in place. Start by reading this book!.... A truly valuable resource that will help business leaders make sense of what people analytics is, why it's crucial, and how to go about building it into your organization. A must read!.... Jenny is one of the world's top minds when it comes to data and people analytics. She has created a valuable resource that every business leader needs to read. If you want to build an organization that is prepared for the future of work then you need to do based on people data. Start by reading this book!"

—Jacob Morgan, author of *The Employee Experience Advantage (2017), The Future of Work (2014) and The Collaborative Organization (2012),* speaker and futurist

"The combination of story-telling, explaining concepts, and illuminating practical application is really quite compelling. This is an increasingly important space—the industry has been on a journey to embrace the available depth of information and transform it into a tool to help all aspects of our businesses. Jenny and David do an amazing job illustrating how modern data analytics can be applied to the HR function, and how this creates a broader impact to a company—empowering HR as a strategic asset to the business. They take a technology space that is relatively new and remove the mystery from it and make it understandable, tangible, and something that can be put into practice."

—Quentin Clark, software executive, advisor, investor, limited partner

"One of the most profound changes in business today is the vast amount of people-related data we have to analyze. This book will help HR and line managers understand their opportunity to apply analytics to many of the people decisions we make every day."

—Josh Bersin, industry analyst, principal and founder, Bersin by Deloitte

"At the heart of *The Data-Driven Leader* is a simple yet powerful insight: that the best way to unleash the collective power of an organization is to unlock the full potential of individual employees working in concert. By connecting data analytics with the rapidly evolving practice of human resources, Jenny Dearborn and David Swanson have created a guide to driving business value that every leader—and not just those in HR—should read."

"At the convergence of people and technology there exists a great opportunity for talent development leaders to shape the future of their organizations. Data analytics are key to that effort, and in this book Jenny and David provide a practical guide for how to measure what really matters and use the information to transform business."

"Opinions are interesting but insight based on data are what leaders really need. 'What happened' 'Why did it happen?' 'What might happen?' 'What should we do?' Answering these four questions effectively is what results driven leaders do. And more than ever, answering all four of them must be based on data and true insight; NOT just gut feel. Organizations are often data rich and insight poor. That state exists is because leaders often avoid the hard work of the hard work. Having the discipline and skill to run an insight driven business is just that: darn hard work. And the current expectation is that 'Human Resource' leaders (CHROs, CPOs, etc.) have the skill and tenacity to be data driven leaders in parallel to the same expectations for profit/loss leaders.

So how does a data driven Chief Human Resource leader act? Well in perfect timing to meet the needs of current 'People Leaders' everywhere, Jenny Dearborn and David Swanson have co-authored *The Data Driven Leader*. The book's protagonist is a newly minted CHRO, Pam Sharp, and she leads a company transformation through the most thoughtful application of data. The authors do a superb job of demonstrating how Pam Sharp and her HR team navigate the most profound business challenges with insight. The narrative of the book gives us a story to embrace and hence specific examples to learn from. Buy *The*

Data Driven Leader and benefit from the rich narrative. Pam Sharp takes you step by step through the world of insight development. She shows that what's in the way is the way? Follow Pam Sharp and we all might find the better route to becoming true data driven leaders!"

—Lorne Rubis, chief evangelist, ATB Financial, Edmonton, CANADA

"*The Data Driven Leader* is an essential guide for leaders who want to navigate complexity with brilliance and win in the new game of work. This insight-packed book will show you how to ask the right questions, gather intelligence and enable your team to find the best answers."

—Liz Wiseman, New York Times bestselling author of
Multipliers and Rookie Smarts, founder, The Wiseman Group

"A good read for HR professionals planning to embark on analytics and don't know where and how to start! I like how the book provided alternative perspectives to the performance indicators that HR departments are tracking currently and practical approaches to leveraging analytics to create solutions to add value to the business."

—Aileen Tan, Group CHRO, Singtel, SINGAPORE

"Anecdotes or Analytics. *The Data Driven Leader* gives voice to this choice that we all make daily in our decision-making process to recruit and retain, motivate and mentor, top talent that will be the best fit for each of our organizations. Crisp, concise and compelling in her writing style, Jenny Dearborn delivers a book that—from cover-to-cover—is a must read for those of us determined to make a difference through the role of HR in our organizations."

—Carl Guardino, president & CEO, Silicon Valley Leadership Group

JENNY DEARBORN
DAVID SWANSON

THE

DATADRIVEN

LEADER

A POWERFUL APPROACH TO
DELIVERING MEASURABLE
BUSINESS IMPACT

THROUGH

PEOPLE ANALYTICS

WILEY

To my amazing husband, John Tarlton, and our awesome, nutty, brilliant kids. I love our crazy life. Servons, Jenny

To my lovely wife, Suzanne Swanson, who supported, reviewed, and encouraged all the way, and to our seven fantastic children. Cheers, David

CONTENTS

ACKNOWLEDGMENTS

We are so thankful and lucky to have assembled a fantastic team of talented professionals to support this book project.

- Deb Arnold—When not pulling content from us like teeth and beautifully weaving everything together in plain English, Deb is the principal of Deb Arnold, Ink., and an expert at winning awards and other recognition for learning and talent thought leaders. Deb is the spirit guide for this effort. Thank you for this and for your partnership over these many, many years—wouldn't be here without you. Find her at www.debarnoldink.com.

- Sergey Feldman, PhD—Subject-matter expert; helped craft the exposition of analytical models, algorithms, and logic. Sergey is head of a cutting-edge machine learning and data science consulting company. We are awed by your genius—thank you for your dedication to our project. Find Sergey at www.data-cowboys.com.

- Joel Freedman—Researcher extraordinaire, dedicated to helping organizations achieve measurable research, leadership development, and conflict resolution results. Joel artfully weaves research into our narrative, grounding us in facts and evidence. He is a joy to work with, and we deeply thank him for his indispensable contributions. Find Joel at GetStarted@FreedmanResearch.com.

- Filipe Muffoletto—Filipe is a Graphics God, Artistic Avenger, Whiteboard Wizard. He is fast, talented, amazing beyond articulation. . . . Find Filipe at fmuffoletto@gmail.com.

- Sanchita Sur—A performance analytics expert, speaker, and published author, Sanchita is the founder of Emplay, an award-winning artificial intelligence (AI) and bot technology firm that helps companies drive better results by providing data driven action recommendations and autonomous execution capabilities. Her HR analytics work inspired much of this book, and its creation was made possible by her many contributions and guidance. Sanchita has patent-pending "Sales DNA" algorithms for accurate sales predictions and prescriptive action plans. To learn more about Emplay, visit www.emplay.net.

PREFACE

In today's workplace, the pace and nature of change are simply unprecedented. So much of what we know about jobs and work is shifting beneath our feet due to powerful forces like robotics, big data, artificial intelligence, the Internet of Things, the sharing economy, the gig economy, and others. World Economic Forum Founder Klaus Schwab calls this the Fourth Industrial Revolution, with technologies so transformative that they are challenging what it means to be human.[1]

It is urgent that we human resource professionals step up our game in response, and effectively prepare for the future. With 47 percent of jobs currently performed by humans potentially eliminated as early as 2030[2] (or 50 percent of work activities disposable right now, according to a more dire prediction[3]), we must change the way *we* think and work. Our profession has evolved from administrative experts in Personnel or Industrial Relations to today's top CHROs—key executives driving measurable business performance. We are encouraged by our collective progress, but also know that HR has much further to go.

Embracing data analytics is key to advancing as a profession and successfully transitioning our organizations into the future. Josh Bersin, a foremost HR thought leader, identifies people analytics as a top HR development: "This new function is critically important and of very high value—just as marketing departments analyze the results of campaigns, create personas and segments of the customer population, and understand the drivers of market share success, we can now do the same thing for our employees."[4]

It is challenging but essential to change our mindsets. Intuition and emotional intelligence, once the hallmarks of successful CHROs and HR professionals, are no longer sufficient. We must now be anchored in data and analytics. But this is good news! Integrating a new analytical approach into our work will make our key capabilities even more powerful. We can deepen our ability to determine root causes and predict the outcomes of programs, not just oversee their implementation.

Whether you seek practical approaches to beginning your analytics journey or additional insights to further develop your analytics efforts, this book is for you. Our goal is to inform, motivate, and inspire you to combine the power of data and analytics with your HR expertise, thus enabling you to more effectively use your organization's most precious resources: your people's time and energy.

A CRITICAL TIME—AND OPPORTUNITY— FOR CHANGE

Studies show that, although many CEOs feel talent is a top competitive differentiator, an increasing number aren't sure they have the employees they need to succeed now or in the future.[5] Worse yet, they don't feel their human resources organizations are equipped to help.[6] It's no wonder we see more CHROs replaced by executives from marketing, operations, or finance—disciplines that have been using data and analytics for years to drive their operations and outcomes. We must rise to the challenge, designing data driven people strategies, and the programs to achieve them, as catalysts for change and transformation.

This starts with changing how we think about metrics and measurement. Too much HR reporting uses only *descriptive analytics*, which capture what has happened: number of people hired, time to fill requisitions, and employee engagement scores are all examples of these "rear view mirror" metrics. We need to move toward diagnosing the "why" behind these metrics, using *diagnostic analytics*, or, in the case of *predictive analytics*, what might happen. Once we quantify these metrics, we can act, guided by *prescriptive analytics*.

Moving from simple reports to predicting the future is a crucial journey we all must take, and the time to start is now.

ANALYTICS IN ACTION

Here's an example. You want to improve hiring results. Your best hiring managers reliably bring in high performers who become more productive more quickly than their peers. You want to identify what those hiring managers do differently and train your other people managers to do the same. How can you build a business case for such an endeavor?

Here's one approach. Partnering with an analytics expert, your finance team and a line of business such as sales, measure the benefits of hiring stronger candidates (for example, faster time to productivity, higher sales, lower attrition) versus the costs of weaker hires. Then, studying the profiles of top performing hires, predict what kind of job candidates will be most successful. Finally, using prescriptive analytics, introduce a program designed to hire people who are X percent more likely to stay, Y percent more likely to reach productivity faster than the average hire, and provide a Z percent higher level of customer satisfaction than the average hire. This approach and these data position your training program for hiring managers as driving business performance, a language every executive speaks.

Throughout this book, we introduce business challenges like the hiring example above, then propose business solutions using sound human resources practices coupled with analytics. While reading *The Data Driven Leader*, imagine the possibilities for people analytics at your company.

WHAT YOU CAN EXPECT FROM THIS BOOK

To make this book accessible, enjoyable to read, informative, and practical, we begin each chapter with a fictional narrative, based on analytics programs we and our teams have developed. We then offer insights and practical suggestions related to that chapter's plot in a commentary section. The fictional company, Exalted Enterprises, represents a realistic composite of the many organizations we have come to know over our careers, including Borland, Business Objects, Chevron, Hewlett-Packard, Interwise, KPMG, Kroger, Microsoft, Motorola, Nordstrom, Oracle, Salesforce.com, SAP, Starbucks, SuccessFactors, Sun Microsystems, T-Mobile, Verizon, and others. As a result, you will likely be able to relate to the concepts, themes, issues, challenges, and characters.

You may identify with our fictional protagonist, Pam Sharp, the new chief human resources officer of Exalted, as she helps turn around her company amidst intense pressures. You'll likely recognize colleagues, past or present, in Elke, Marcus, Martha, and Sameer, Pam's leadership team. We aim to portray an organization and a team like yours, which, with the application of people analytics, will hopefully experience similar triumphs.

Although the approaches they take are applicable to any aspect of a business, we focus on sales because about 80 percent of any company is typically involved with some aspect of sales, so a sales-focused initiative will usually attract significant buy-in across the organization. Once you have implemented people analytics for sales, you can replicate your initiatives in other areas.

The book that inspired this one, *Data Driven: How Performance Analytics Delivers Extraordinary Sales Results*,[7] also stars Pam Sharp, who leverages analytics to understand and triumphantly overhaul sales at Trajectory, an Exalted subsidiary. *The Data Driven Leader* brings Pam back as Exalted's CHRO, using HR analytics as a prism through which to view the ways data can transform how leaders think about and solve business challenges.

GETTING STARTED

Dive in and discover the world of analytics. Use data to drive measurable business outcomes, prepare the workforce of the future, and be a key participant in driving the strategy and sustainability of your organization.

As Mark Twain is often quoted: "The best way to get ahead is to get started." We hope this book will inspire you to start or to energize and advance the work you have already begun.

We wish you tremendous success.

Jenny Dearborn and David Swanson

NOTES

1. Klaus Schwab, *The Fourth Industrial Revolution* (New York: Crown Business, 2017).
2. Carl Benedict Frey and Michael A. Osborne, "The Future of Employment: How Susceptible Are Jobs to Computerization?" (Unpublished paper, Oxford Martin School, University of Oxford, September 17, 2013), accessed May 25, 2017. http://www.oxfordmartin.ox.ac.uk/downloads/academic/The_Future_of_Employment.pdf.
3. James Manyika, Michael Chui, Mehdi Miremadi, Jacques Bughin, Katy George, Paul Willmott, and Martin Dewhurst, "Harnessing Automation for a Future That Works" *McKinsey Global Institute Report* (January 2017), accessed May 25, 2017. http://www.mckinsey.com/global-themes/digital-disruption/harnessing-automation-for-a-future-that-works.
4. Josh Bersin, *Predictions for 2016: A Bold New World of Talent, Learning, Leadership, and HR Technology Ahead* (Oakland,

CA: Bersin by Deloitte), 37, accessed May 25, 2017. https://www2.deloitte.com/content/dam/Deloitte/at/Documents/human-capital/bersin-predictions-2016.pdf.

5. ManpowerGroup, *2016/2017 Talent Shortage Survey* (Milwaukee, WI: ManpowerGroup, 2017), accessed May 25, 2017. http://www.manpowergroup.us/campaigns/talent-shortage/assets/pdf/2016-Talent-Shortage-Infographic.pdf; PwC, *Global CEO Survey: The Talent Challenge* (London: PwC, 2014), accessed May 25, 2017. http://www.pwc.com/gx/en/hr-management-services/publications/assets/ceosurvey-talent-challenge.pdf.

6. Oxford Economics, *Workforce 2020: The Looming Talent Crisis* (New York: Oxford Economics, September 2014), accessed May 25, 2017. https://www.oxfordeconomics.com/publication/open/250945.

7. Jenny Dearborn, *Data Driven: How Performance Analytics Delivers Extraordinary Results* (Hoboken, NJ: Wiley, 2015).

Chapter 1

PLAYING THE BLAME GAME

The winter sun shone spectacularly over Lake Michigan, reflecting Pam Sharp's buoyant mood. She loved a thorny business problem promising big risk and an even bigger pay-off, and after a week on the job, she was ready to dive in. From her new office on the 23rd floor, she had an expansive view of both the lake and downtown Chicago, now dusted with a light coating of January snow. She smiled to herself as she imagined the 70-degree weather back in Palo Alto, but Pam knew she'd made the right move.

Pam never expected to become the chief human resources officer of Exalted Industries. With a meteoric career in sales, she had been recruited to Trajectory Systems, an Exalted subsidiary in Silicon Valley, as its chief sales officer. Weak revenues had threatened the company's survival, and Trajectory CEO David Craig had brought her in to turn things around. A chance meeting with a young data whiz led Pam and her team to embark on a series of data analytics initiatives, transforming sales enablement. In a relatively short time, the company was back on track to hit its revenue targets, and David Craig was promoted to CEO of Exalted.

After just a year leading Exalted, David had flown Pam to Chicago for a mysterious dinner meeting, revealing that the company faced more serious challenges than he'd expected: revenue was down, as were margins, customer satisfaction ratings, and the stock price. The media was extolling competitors' innovations, while Exalted, although still the market leader, hadn't launched a new product in three years, instead making several acquisitions that were only moderately successful. Making matters worse, attrition was up, with some high-profile exits. The competition was taking both customers and an alarming number of top sales reps.

Pam had been caught off-guard—something she rarely experienced—when David offered her the role of CHRO.

"I'm flattered, David, of course," she said, "but why would a new HR leader be the answer to Exalted's challenges? And why wouldn't you fill the role with an experienced HR professional?"

"I'll answer your first question first. Losing key talent is part of it," David explained, "but I also can't ignore my leaders across the company who point fingers at HR when they talk about our problems. Sales jobs are going unfilled for months at a time, and our best reps are leaving just when we need them most. The latest employee engagement survey scores show morale at an all-time low, especially in Sales. And we're desperate for fresh talent to get new products to market, but Talent Acquisition just isn't bringing in the innovators we need."

"I can't imagine that any one department could be the source of *all* the company's problems," Pam countered.

"True," continued David, "but I appreciate now that everything comes down to having the right people and, to answer your second question, I sense that, under a motivational leader with strong business savvy, which you have in spades, HR could help tease out and solve many of our issues. Besides, I've seen what you can do with analytics, and we need more data driven decision making at Exalted. Too much is determined by gut, not facts. You're the right leader, Pam, to help not only fix what's broken but also to change our culture to be more data-centric."

Then David raised the stakes. "You should know that if key business metrics don't start improving, and quickly, we'll both be out of a job. Our chief sales officer isn't making things easy. I think you know Bobby Cash. He's continually griping about how everyone else is to blame for sagging sales, especially HR. He'll take aim at you for sure."

Pam smiled, recalling Bobby's bravado, Southern drawl, and flashy watches. "Sure, I know Bobby from quarterly sales meetings and annual sales kickoffs. He's a decent guy, although his attitude toward women in business is from the dark ages. I can handle him."

"One last thorn in my side, and soon yours," David cautioned her, "is an activist board member, Thomas Ashcroft. He's very experienced, but since he sold his last business he's made us the key beneficiaries of his 'hard-earned' wisdom. The guy walks around with a travel mug that says, 'Retired: I know everything and have all the time in the world to tell you about it.' He'll no doubt be on your doorstep soon, full of advice. He fancies himself quite the mentor. In fact, through a board/C-suite mentor match, he's made himself invaluable to our chief marketing officer, Anne Rodriguez. You'll like her. She's tough and smart. Unfortunately, while I know Ashcroft has the best interests of Anne *and* Exalted at heart, I'm not always sure his guidance is on target."

"The last and most important piece of information you need," David said, leaning in and looking her straight in the eye, "is the overall engagement survey feedback, which we're keeping confidential for now. Many employees said they don't believe in the company anymore, but for different reasons. Some said we're a dinosaur, behind the times, afraid to innovate and develop new products. Others said the opposite: we're moving too quickly and abandoning our legacy by acquiring new products. There's some deep-seated unhappiness, and we need to get to the bottom of it."

David's warnings had only made the opportunity more compelling. After persuading her family to move to Chicago— in the middle of a school year, in the dead of winter, from California!—Pam began preparing for her new role. Always an excellent student, she read voraciously about her new domain: books, articles, reports, and more on HR and human capital analytics. She even discovered that she was part of a trend—CEOs bringing in a leader with P&L experience to head their HR departments, to boost their strategic capabilities and impact.

She had hoped that her new team and peers knew about this trend. That might quell some of the anxieties she imagined they'd have about a sales executive becoming their leader and the CHRO. Unfortunately, based on her first week at Exalted, meeting with her C-suite peers and direct reports, that turned out to be spectacularly optimistic.

Yet she'd never failed at anything, and didn't intend to start now. She was confident that she'd succeed, winning over her employees, colleagues and any activist investor who crossed her path.

She just didn't yet know exactly how.

ENTERING THE FRAY

That afternoon, she and her team began their day-and-a-half strategic planning off-site a few blocks away from headquarters. Gathered in the spacious room, surrounded on three sides by whiteboards, were Marcus Long, VP of HR Business Partners; Sameer Mahal, VP of HR Shared Services; Elke Andersen, VP of Talent Acquisition; and Martha Lee, VP of HR Centers of Excellence (Talent Strategy, Total Rewards, Leadership Development, Diversity/Inclusion, and Learning & Development).

After some opening remarks to her staff, Pam dove right in: "We're facing very serious challenges as a company. At this off-site I want us to start thinking as a leadership team about how we will address these challenges. Here's the overview I got from David."

Pam displayed a PowerPoint slide on the screen.

REVENUE	⬇ **18%** (−$360M)
MARGINS	⬇ **22%**
STOCK PRICE	⬇ **25%**
CUSTOMER NPS	⬇ **20%** ALL-TIME LOW
% REVENUE FROM NET NEW PRODUCTS	**< 10%**
SALES ATTRITION	⬆ **38%**

"The numbers tell a pretty dismal story. And yet, the board has given David a goal of double-digit growth by the end of the year, in keeping with the average growth rate for the healthiest companies in our industry. Help this newcomer out. What do we think is going on here?" Pam asked, with a tone that communicated she was looking to gain information, not place blame.

Her team uncomfortably shifted in their seats, glancing at one another.

"Any theories? Hunches? Facts? Rumors?" Pam asked with an encouraging smile.

No one smiled in return. "Well," began Marcus Long, taking a deep breath and adjusting the sleeves on his neatly tailored black blazer, "only the last two items on that list, about attrition, have anything to do with HR, and they're pretty much caused by the first five. Among us here, I think people are jumping off what they see as a sinking ship. Some of the latest engagement survey results are so bad that we're keeping them confidential, as I'm sure David told you. Employees are saying they don't believe in our leadership or the direction of the company."

"That's right," interjected Martha Lee, nervously playing with her string of pearls. "People are demoralized, so they're seeking greener pastures elsewhere. I just wish our executives cared more and gave us budget to address it. They even downsized our holiday party this past December. How is that going to help us keep people? And besides, attrition may be at an all-time high for Exalted, but we're still close to the industry average. We're doing *our* jobs."

Elke Andersen cleared her throat and tucked a strand of her blonde hair behind her ear. "It's no wonder our best people are leaving, given how little innovation is happening here. How could I be expected to attract new talent when we aren't putting out new products? Never mind that I am continually dealing with the revolving door of sales reps. We'll never get revenues up if Sales doesn't stop driving away everyone my team brings in."

Pam glanced over at Sameer Mahal, who hadn't yet spoken. "Sameer?" she asked, raising an expectant eyebrow.

"I'm with them," said Sameer in his crisp British accent. "HR gets blamed for everything, but most of the company's problems have nothing to do with us. We are working harder than ever, but we never receive sufficient resources."

Marcus, Elke, and Martha nodded, clearly dejected.

"Guys," said Pam gently, "that kind of attitude won't fly anymore. We need to think more like our business owners and how we can help them solve their problems. That's especially true for Sales, which needs to be successful if Exalted is going to pull through this crisis. I've certainly heard plenty from Bobby Cash on that subject already. For right now, let's get our own house in order. My peers on Exalted's leadership team have told me what they believe is wrong with our HR organization. I'd like to know what you think."

"Well," Marcus began cautiously as others again shifted uncomfortably in their seats, "Sales is definitely an issue. As Bobby's HR business partner, I know he has a lot of complaints, and unfortunately, I think some of them are justified.

He keeps asking me why it takes up to eight months to fill a Sales rep role and I don't have answers."

"I wish you wouldn't always take his side, Marcus," said Elke defensively. "Bobby's hiring managers are to blame here. They're too picky and too slow. Good candidates don't want to go through umpteen interviews, and they get snatched up by our competitors. By the time our hiring managers make up their minds, we get the worst candidates, who fail and leave and then we need to start all over again. And some hiring managers have the nerve to complain that we're not getting them the right candidates when they give us vague job postings."

"Hold on Elke," said Marcus, equally defensive. "I'm not trying to take sides. We all know Bobby can be abrasive. He's a great guy but a tough client. He tells it like it is, and that's hard to hear, but we've got to listen. Think about the repercussions of our hiring challenges. The reps we *do* have are struggling to keep up, and so managers jump in and spend more time in the field, which means they aren't around to coach the new hires. It's a mess."

"If you want Bobby off your back, maybe you should tell him how our Talent Acquisition department meets or exceeds every industry benchmark for key performance metrics," Elke insisted. "Our time to post is only five business days, and we get fifteen candidates for every open position—that's three times the industry average! I hate to say it, but things could move faster if Sameer's people would get offer letters out right away."

Marcus, growing irritated, looked at Pam, who nodded to him to continue. Dozens of one-on-one meetings could never yield the kind of insights this discussion was surfacing. "Sameer, is that true?" Marcus asked. "We get plenty of complaints about how long it takes to get new hires badges and laptops. I didn't know there were *also* problems with offer letters."

"Elke, how can you blame me?" exclaimed Sameer, straightening up in his seat. "We can only dispatch offers when *your* team sends us the information. That's also the problem with badges and laptops: you don't give us enough lead time. Our Service Level Agreement clearly states that we must have at least seven business days to respond to a new hire request, and we have had demands for turnarounds as short as from Friday afternoon to Monday morning. I don't have teams working over the weekend!"

Elke shook her head repeatedly. "Sameer, this is *Bobby's* fault. Just dealing with the Sales attrition mess has us totally over-extended. We can't possibly keep up. And then your team messes up an offer letter and *we* take the blame."

Sameer's graying moustache began to twitch. "Elke, you only deal with incoming hires. We get them coming and going. All this churn is killing my team. It seems like all we ever do is process terminations and new hires for Sales. The final checks, the COBRA set-up, the equipment return—I could go on and on. How can we possibly deliver a quality employee experience under these circumstances?"

"You can complain all you like about Bobby, but without Sales, Exalted would come to a grinding halt," Marcus declared, his voice rising. "And as much as we *all* say that HR doesn't get respect, we have to earn it. When we can't nail the basics, like making sure people have correct offer letters and the right equipment on their first day of work, it makes us all look bad. Only *I'm* the one who takes the heat for it in Bobby's weekly staff meetings."

"That's just it," exclaimed Sameer. "These things would be basics except we're working with old systems and unrealistic timelines. And then we're scolded when we can't deliver. Marcus, you know how these executives can get. They have you request endless urgent reports from me, and we move mountains to chase down data—but for what purpose? It's demoralizing to jump at every fire drill and never even know what you do with the data. And I've got people jumping ship from Global Shared Services for better paid jobs in Finance. Martha, can't you please give me a decent comp budget? And maybe give Sales better comp? And training? Maybe then reps will stop quitting to go to the competition and we can get off this bloody hamster wheel!"

Sameer's outburst took Martha by surprise. "Well, Sameer, I never knew how much this upset you," she said, swiveling her chair slowly in his direction and trying to remain calm. "But tell me, how can I deliver new hire training if the new hires don't have their laptops? People are always late to New Hire Orientation because they're filling out forms you should have sent them weeks earlier. With a new hire experience like that, it's not surprising that they don't stick around."

"Martha, I'm sorry to say, Sameer is right about compensation," Marcus interjected. "Our financial performance isn't exactly a secret, and the press has been fawning over our rivals as innovators, even though they're obviously selling snake oil. We need to offer more attractive comp packages to get top talent."

"Well, Marcus," Martha huffed, "our comp is at or above market. Our Total Rewards people are the best in the business, and you know how fussy they are about considering every detail in their calculations. I'm certain we're competitive. And you know what else? If reps actually *went* to training they might have a chance at meeting quota. Sales leadership doesn't care, so no one makes them go. Or they go and someone yanks them out in the middle to send them back into the field. We worked so hard to put together a new enablement curriculum, but is anyone using it? No. And new reps continue to struggle. We try to do everything the executives tell us, and still they're not satisfied. This is a thankless grind. I'm exhausted just thinking about it."

Marcus, Elke, and Sameer all began talking at once, their voices rising in frustration.

Pam Sharp, all 5 feet 11 inches of her, rose to speak. "All right, everyone," she said firmly, "thank you for playing what I call The Blame Game. You've just given me a very enlightening education about what's going wrong around here, and only one thing is for sure."

All eyes were fixed on their new CHRO.

"Starting right now," said Pam, "we focus on understanding and fixing problems. We'll never make progress or gain the respect of our senior leaders by throwing around accusations or blaming each other. We need to understand the *why*. Why are these breakdowns happening, especially if we have such great KPIs that beat industry standards? It doesn't make sense that our key measurements would be green if all the business results are red. Until we understand WHY we are experiencing these challenges, we won't fix a thing, and we won't serve our ultimate customers—Exalted employees."

Pam walked over to one of the whiteboards and started to draw. "We also need to start thinking differently about our role at Exalted. Here's a sketch of a value chain to show you what I mean."

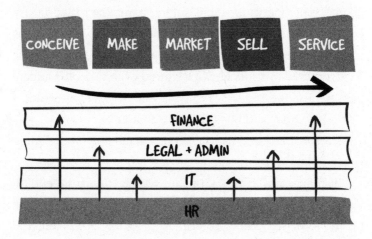

"For a company to excel," Pam explained, "each of the activities here must succeed. If Exalted is to be successful, then we must be successful, and the same goes for our support colleagues in Finance, IT, and elsewhere. We are critical to our company's future, and we need to think of ourselves and our roles that way."

"And besides," she continued, "at each stage of the value chain, *people* must excel. If people fail, the company fails. So, if we're supplying the people and they're not performing, we need to do things differently. And we must partner with any and every part of the business to do so. We can't have an us versus them mentality."

"I understand your perspective, Pam," said Marcus, nodding pensively. "I hear this from my executives and my HRBP team all the time. But it's a big leap from this theoretical drawing to an actual plan of how to make it happen, especially when we can't directly influence business outcomes."

"I'm sorry, but I don't get it," Martha frowned. "We're just doing what the business owners tell us to. Don't they know what they need from us?"

"Pam, I'm very concerned about how my team is going to close HR Service Center tickets if we've got the success of the company on our shoulders," Sameer said quietly.

Elke stared at Pam. "But . . . how . . . many people will I need to hire now?"

Pam smiled gently at her new team, imagining the end of the journey they were just beginning. "I wouldn't have taken this job if I weren't convinced that I could get us where we need to go. I know we'll get there, and we'll leave behind the days of being order-takers. We will transform HR into an organization that drives strategic business impact, and we'll get that seat at the strategic table. For now, on to the evening's surprise activity. I did a little homework and found out you're all Bulls fans, so I arranged for us to go watch tonight's game from the corporate box. They just happen to be playing my hometown team, the Golden State Warriors." Pam had a hunch they'd need a strong finish to the day.

As the team gathered their belongings, Marcus whispered to Elke, "Well, this should be interesting. I think Bobby is headed there as well with some of our key customer accounts."

"I'd like to see how convinced Pam is about our success when it's Bobby Cash breathing down *her* neck," Elke replied quietly, following the others out the door.

SUMMARY

Pam Sharp, who successfully used data analytics to transform revenue as chief sales officer at Trajectory Systems, is now the new chief human resources officer at Trajectory's parent company, Exalted Industries. Exalted's situation is dire: revenues, margins, customer satisfaction ratings, and stock price are down, while attrition is up. With no new product launched in three years, Exalted risks losing its market-leading position.

The board has tasked CEO David Craig and his executive team, including his new hire, Pam, to drive double-digit growth by year-end. Asked by Pam for insights about the company's precarious position, her new team members instead blame colleagues and each other. Pam rallies her staff to focus on problem solving versus blame casting and to appreciate the importance of HR as a strategic function. She is confident they'll get there.

COMMENTARY

A NEW ERA FOR HR

Human Resource professionals have unprecedented opportunities, not only to craft data driven people strategies that will generate measurable business impact, but also to lead their companies' digital transformation and facilitate a smooth transition into the future world of work. But too few HR organizations have the command of data analytics this leadership requires. Too *many* have few or no analytics capabilities. For these reasons and others, CEOs are increasingly seeking business leaders to take on the CHRO role, valuing business acumen—especially experience using analytics to improve business performance—over traditional HR domain knowledge.

Exalted CEO David Craig is a perfect example. He recruits Pam Sharp because she is a smart and experienced business leader, but also because she has a track record of using data to drive revenue improvement, exactly what Exalted needs to achieve double-digit growth. Pam immediately demonstrates Craig's wisdom by seeking to first understand Exalted's corporate pains, not simply its HR woes.

Her HR leadership team, however, is still inwardly focused and, without the benefit of data driven decision making, Pam's questions about the company's troubles soon lead to a "blame game": Marcus (VP HR), Elke (VP Talent Acquisition), Martha (VP HR Centers of Excellence), and Sameer (VP, Global Shared Services) point fingers at their business stakeholders and then at each other, rather than trying to understand the root causes behind Exalted's challenges. This scenario is all too common.

Pam shows strong leadership skills by listening patiently to her new team, yielding invaluable insights into their self-perceptions and interpersonal dynamics. This gives her an opening to start shifting their mindsets about their roles and importance at Exalted. Pam rightly points out the need to understand the gap between seemingly great HR outcomes (for example, the key performance statistics that Elke and Martha cite) and Exalted's dismal corporate outcomes.

She also presents a radical notion for this team: that HR can, and must, drive business outcomes. She sketches a simplified version of Michael Porter's value chain, described in the business guru's 1985 best-seller, *Competitive Advantage: Creating and Sustaining Superior Performance* (a closer version to the original appears on the next page).[1] Porter puts forth that *each* of a business's five key primary activities and four support activities—including HR—are critical to profitability.

In Human Resources, we often feel so much pressure that we default to thinking we only impact our own programs. Yet, as Pam so clearly points out, if we are responsible for hiring, developing, and retaining our people, then we have a fundamental role in the success or failure of the business.

Marcus agrees but draws a blank on how to turn theory into practice. Martha has fully absorbed the order-taker mentality and expects the business to direct her. Sameer's immediate concern is how to be strategic *and* fulfill what he sees as his key role: close HR service tickets. Similarly, Elke is immediately concerned about additional hiring burdens.

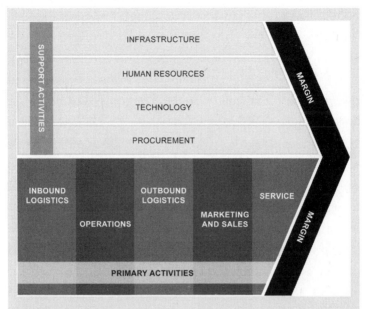

Figure 1c.1 Michael Porter's Value Chain

Adapted from Michael E. Porter, *Competitive Advantage: Creating and Sustaining Superior Performance* (New York: The Free Press, 1985).

These predictable reactions are very real psychological obstacles that HR organizations must overcome. For Pam to be successful at her primary goals—increasing Exalted revenue and moving it toward being a company of data driven leaders—she must first transform her own team's mentality from order-takers to strategic business partners. This could prove even more challenging than winning over her executive peers. Many of these considerations are likely important at your company as well.

NOT ANALYTICS-SAVVY? YOU'RE NOT ALONE

According to recent research, 71 percent of companies think HR data analytics is an organizational priority, but fewer than one in ten report having usable data.[2] Another recent study reported that more than one-third of companies don't use data in any decision making.[3]

And even those who do don't do so very effectively. A survey conducted by PwC found that three in four companies were held back by issues including corporate culture and regulatory roadblocks or just didn't know what value their information might offer, and so obtained little or no tangible benefit from their data.[4]

Yet, as you will read, there are many benefits to using HR analytics. Deftly capturing and analyzing data can enable HR to increase engagement, predict and stem attrition, enhance hiring, and much more.

Further, by not leveraging data analytics or doing so without the right guidance, HR organizations severely limit their ability to solve problems and advance business strategies. Risks include:

- **Decision making by gut, not fact:** Common sense can sometimes be our enemy. Why? Because sense and logic can be deeply personal and subjective. Data, however, can remove guesswork, biases, anecdotal reasoning, and other human foibles that can throw strategic efforts off course. Data can also take the emotion out of business discussions and break down silos as objective metrics light the way forward.

- **Solving the wrong problem:** You've surely been there— weeks or months of effort to resolve a vexing challenge are revealed to have been a waste of time, resources, and good will because the challenge turned out to be a misunderstanding, a red herring, or a rush to judgment. Data helps avoid predetermined (and often erroneous) approaches to problem solving.

- **Measuring efficiency rather than effectiveness:** In this chapter, the VP of Talent Acquisition, Elke, points with pride to an average time-to-post of five business days. But is Exalted better served by having jobs posted quickly, or by ensuring that postings are accurate to attract the most appropriate applicants? Our next chapter will take a closer look at how HR teams can revisit the metrics they're capturing to ensure a focus on effectiveness and not just efficiency.

Too many companies, and HR functions, don't focus on defining and achieving measurable outcomes that align with and advance business strategy. That's where we find Exalted's HR team today—but not for long.

Pam's 3 Key Ideas, Boiled Down:

1 If we focus only on HR, we won't get a seat at the strategic table. We need to focus on the whole company.

2 HR needs to own business problems because companies can only function with people, and we bring the people.

3 We can only accomplish this with data guiding us.

Figure 1c.2 Pam's Three Key Ideas

NOTES

1. Michael E. Porter, *Competitive Advantage: Creating and Sustaining Superior Performance* (New York: The Free Press, 1985).

2. Laurence Collins, Dave Fineman, and Akio Tsuchida, "People Analytics: Recalculating the Route." In Bill Pelster and Jeff Schwartz (eds.), *Global Human Capital Trends 2017* (Westlake, TX: Deloitte University Press), accessed May 25, 2017, https://dupress.deloitte.com/content/dam/dup-us-en/articles/HCTrends_2017/DUP_Global-Human-capital-trends_2017.pdf.

3. "Marketing's Moment: Leading Disruption," *Association of National Advertisers*, last modified October 16, 2014, accessed May 25, 2017, http://www.ana.net/content/show/id/32226.

4. Claire Reid, Richard Petley, Julie McLean, Kieran Jones, and Peter Ruck, *Seizing the Information Advantage: How Organizations Can Unlock Value and Insight from the Information They Hold* (London: PwC/Iron Mountain, September 2015), accessed May 25, 2017, http://www.ironmountain.com/Knowledge -Center/Reference-Library/View-by-Document-Type/White -Papers-Briefs/S/Seizing-The-Information-Advantage-Executive -Summary.aspx.

Chapter 2

LEADING WITH BUSINESS OUTCOMES

The United Center, on West Madison in the heart of downtown Chicago, was brightly lit and filled with excited fans
decked out in Chicago Bulls regalia when the new Exalted
CHRO and her leadership team arrived. Marcus had tipped off
Pam about Bobby's likely attendance, but she wasn't about to
let a sales exec ruin her team's good time, especially after the
day's intense discussions. As they headed toward the Exalted
corporate suite, Pam heard a familiar voice.

"Hey, 42!"

Pam smiled and turned to see her college basketball
coach coming toward her with a warm grin and an extended
hand. Well into his sixties, Shep Wheeler looked as fit as ever.
"Coach, what are you doing here?" She knew he was still
coaching at her *alma mater*, Pepperdine, in Malibu.

"I'm scouting high school players at a local tournament.
I had a free evening, and another coach gave me a ticket.
What about you? You're far from home, too."

"Actually, Chicago is home now," Pam said, quickly filling him in on her new role and introducing him to her team
members. "Since you're here on your own, why don't you join
us in the corporate box? I'm sure there's room for one more."

"I'd love to, Pam, thank you," he answered. "Since the last
time we bumped into each other, I've been using data analytics even more—to identify talent, make recruiting decisions,
develop our players. We even have an app to help us. I'll tell
you all about it."

As the group entered the suite, Bobby Cash stood surrounded by executives from one of Exalted's top customers.

"Pam Sharp!" he exclaimed, interrupting himself mid-joke. "How are ya, girl? Gentlemen, this is our new chief human resources officer, Pam Sharp. Her background is in Sales, as you might have heard, but I guess it was time for a role with an easier schedule. You know how it is for ladies with school-age kids."

Pam ignored the barb and held out her hand to the customer's CEO, whom she recognized from her research on Exalted's key accounts. "It's really a pleasure to meet you. I've been following your business and read about your new product release. I think your innovation is going to revolutionize the market. It was fascinating to see how you've used analytics. I'd love to hear more about that."

"That project was my baby," replied the CEO, clearly impressed. "I'd be happy to tell you whatever you want. Let's have lunch."

"That would be terrific," said Pam. "I'll reach out to your office to schedule something."

Bobby flashed his best fake smile. "Let's continue the introductions, shall we?"

As Pam and Bobby introduced their respective parties, the conversation quickly turned to Pam's record as #42 at Pepperdine, the team's last season, and the state of women's college basketball. Bobby barely concealed his displeasure at being sidelined again. "Wait 'til you see the sushi spread we've got for you," he declared, motioning toward the buffet.

As people headed for the food, Bobby cornered Pam. "How come your people are here and not out finding me sales reps?" he challenged. "My guys are out there busting their butts to cover quotas. We owe them better."

"We spent plenty of time talking about that exact subject at our off-site today," said Pam with a smile, determined to stay positive. "I'm confident we'll be able to make the needed changes. In fact, Coach Wheeler was going to share how Pepperdine has been using analytics to find and hire top talent. You might want to listen in."

Just then, the coach walked over, his plate piled high with sushi. "California rolls, in honor of you, Pam," he said, giving her a friendly elbow jab. "You know, you ought to see our talent scout assessment app!" he continued. "We were spending a pile of money tracking how high candidates could jump and how much they scored, but that data didn't always lead us to big winners. This new app takes a 360-degree view, including community involvement and social media—both what they're posting and who they're connected to—things that indicate maturity, which is a huge factor in their success as college players."

"That's a great analogy for what we did with sales reps at Trajectory," said Pam. "We determined what our analytics consultant called the 'DNA' of a great sales rep, all the different components that makes someone successful, and then trained others in those skills and behaviors. The results were amazing."

"I don't need any fancy analytics to know who to hire," scoffed Bobby. "I just look them in the eyes. That tells me who's got the right stuff and who doesn't."

Pam took the high road and kept her tone friendly. "Bobby, not everyone is as good at interviewing as you. Plus, you haven't been happy with the candidates we've sent you, so we clearly need more guidance. I think analytics could help us again."

"Well, at least you're not blaming me like some of your VPs do," Bobby snickered. "That's a good start."

Coach Wheeler, taking Pam's lead, smiled as well. "Bobby, you're right that the human element is always critical. Data analytics is partly about the data but mostly about the analysis—knowing what you're looking for—and once you have it, how to use the data to make decisions," he said, giving Pam a sly wink.

"If you'll excuse me," said Bobby gruffly, "I've got customers to tend to. *They* trust me. Maybe you could extend me the same courtesy."

Just then a roar went up from the crowd. The game was about to begin. As people headed to take their seats, Elke, who'd discretely overheard the entire conversation, thought to herself, "Maybe the new boss isn't as much of a disaster as I thought. If that's how she stands up to Bobby, there's hope yet."

A NEW WAY OF THINKING

At the off-site the next morning, Pam was pleased to see that the team's spirits had lifted. After greeting everyone, grabbing coffee, and sharing some laughs about the game, she began. "OK, everyone. Yesterday, we talked about some very important issues facing us as a company and as an HR department. Today I'd like to talk through some frameworks for resolving these issues so that we can help Exalted achieve that double-digit growth in revenue."

"The first is *design thinking*. There are a few different definitions of design thinking, but the one I tend to find useful is problem solving from a human perspective, with the goal of creating solutions that combine feasibility, viability, and desirability." Pam drew a quick sketch on the whiteboard.

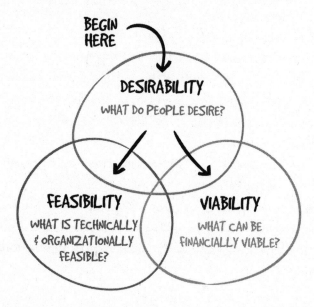

"The starting point is building empathy by putting yourself in the shoes of your customer," she continued, "which cultivates an understanding of *desirability*. It makes sense to first think about what the end-user wants, and then explore what's viable and feasible. Let's start by applying the idea of desirability to some of our processes. Since hiring is a key issue, I'd like to start there, and problem solve together as a team. Elke, OK if we enter your world for a bit? This should give you a head start on getting Bobby off your back."

Elke took a deep breath, quieted her internal anxiety, and nodded in agreement. Having witnessed Pam stand up for the team at the game, Elke wanted to give her a chance.

"Fantastic," said Pam, "thank you." Pam walked over to one of the room-length whiteboards. "I'll take notes. Let's start with the candidate experience. Putting ourselves in the shoes of job hunters, what do they want?"

"We've just done some research on redesigning our career portal, so I've got a pretty good handle on this," Elke offered. "Users want minimal clicks to find information, and to upload a résumé in any format. And Millennials want to be able to send video or other content with their application. Our current portal is not good on those fronts. I just wish we had the budget to actually do the redesign."

"If we can gather data that shows a return on investment, we'll be on our way to having that new portal funded," declared Pam, writing Elke's points on the whiteboard. "What else?"

Sameer chimed in: "Applicants want a quick reply after they respond to a job posting or after they interview. And if they get the job, they want to receive an offer letter right away. Sorry, Elke, that wasn't meant as a jab at you or your team."

"No worries, Sameer," Elke replied with a conciliatory nod.

"I've heard some related feedback," said Marcus. "Candidates referred by an employee want that person to be updated on their progress. The employee wants that, too, but apparently, it's not always the case, and that dissuades employees from making referrals in the future."

Before Elke could object, Pam chimed in. "Marcus, we're just focused on desires for now. Let's leave the fixing for later. What else do job candidates want?"

"Well," said Martha, "my niece is finishing grad school this spring and looking for work. She complains that some career sites don't show what kind of people work at the company and why. That lines up with recent data I've seen saying it's more important to this age group to know who they might work *with* than the brand they might work *for*. I don't mean to stereotype Millennials, but of course she wants to know how the company will give her opportunities to change the world."

"Sounds like your niece is looking for the employee value proposition," said Pam, adding EVP to the list, "the reasons why someone would want to work here."

Her team members looked at each other, all with the same thought: How does this sales guru know so much about HR? "I told you I read up," said Pam with a smile, reading their expressions.

She then drew a thick vertical arrow extending from the list and wrote two words next to it:

"Let's switch gears a bit now, and talk about the hiring manager experience," Pam said, turning back to the group. "What do our hiring managers want?"

Marcus was the first to jump in. "I hear about this all the time so I can rattle off most of the list. They want to hear back right away after posting a job req, they want to interview candidates who are right for the job and fit our diversity objectives, and enough candidates that they can really make a good choice. They also want their top choice to receive an offer letter quickly. And, of course, to accept the offer. And they want the whole process to not take more than a few weeks."

Elke was poised to protest when Marcus added, "Sorry, Elke. I'm just telling you all what I hear." She was feeling deflated but threw up her hands in a good-natured acceptance of his apology. Maybe this would help her fend off Bobby's griping, she thought.

"Unfortunately," Martha began hesitatingly, "one of my directors has been looking for a program manager and he keeps telling me horror stories—I mean, he's been sharing insights about what's important to him in the hiring process."

"Go on," said Elke. "Let's get it all out." Pam smiled to herself as she continued her new list on the whiteboard, encouraged by her team's improving communications.

"He'd like email subject lines to be clearly marked so he knows when he's getting a résumé, for example, even if he doesn't know the sender," Martha explained. "We use a lot of contractors, and sometimes their emails get lost in the shuffle. Also, he really, *really* wants his job description to match the online posting."

"OK, I know I'm not supposed to be discussing fixes at this point," Elke interjected, "but Martha brings up another reason we need to revamp our career portal. The back end is a disaster. Believe it or not, it's hard to update job postings, so to keep things moving quickly, sometimes a recruiter will use a similar one that's already in the system. It's not a great excuse, but it speaks to some of our real challenges."

Pam reassured her, "We'll get to the bottom of this, Elke. Sounds like upgrading our career portal is an important investment if we're going to fix our hiring process. And what we're doing right now is a big step in the right direction." She drew an arrow from the second list and wrote two words next to it:

She stepped away so the group could take in the results of their brief brainstorming.

CANDIDATE EXPERIENCE

HIRING MANAGER EXPERIENCE

MINIMAL CLICKS

UPLOAD RESUME IN ANY FORMAT

SEND VIDEO & OTHER CONTENT

QUICK REPLY TO POSTING, QUICK OFFER LETTER

SENSE OF PURPOSE/ EMPLOYEE VALUE PROP

USER-FRIENDLY

PERSUASIVE

WELL-ORGANIZED

RESULTS-FOCUSED

TIMELY RESPONSES

RIGHT CANDIDATES

CHOICE OF CANDIDATES

CLEARLY MARKED EMAILS

JOB POSTING MATCHES JOB DESCRIPTION

"Elke," Pam began, "I looked at the key performance indicators you've been measured on. Would you say they align with the kind of information we captured just now?"

Elke thought for a moment. "Actually, no. Not at all," she answered. "I'm supposed to fill jobs quickly and cost-effectively."

"Tell me about this disconnect," Pam encouraged Elke.

"My top KPIs start with time to post, from when the hiring manager submits the request to when it's posted online. That's currently five business days. The time from posting to getting a candidate in to interview is also five business days.

Both of those are on par with industry benchmarks. As I mentioned yesterday, our ratio of candidates to open positions is 15x. The industry average is only 5x, so our hiring managers get plenty of choice. And our cost of hiring is low, too. We're not throwing money at candidates like some of our competitors. But very little of that is related to the experiences we've just described."

"Thanks for that, Elke. I appreciate your thoughtful reflection," Pam responded, writing the KPIs on a new list on the whiteboard. "Are there any KPIs we're not doing so well on?"

"Well, sure," Elke admitted, "but they're not our fault. Like I said yesterday, our hiring managers are too picky. That's why our ratio of open reqs to filled positions and our time to fill a role are, well, less than stellar. The rejection rate is high because managers do too many rounds of interviews and candidates lose interest. New employee retention is down because, by the time hiring managers make decisions, the better candidates are gone and they hire people who are less likely to succeed."

Pam finished adding these items, then turned to face the group. "Marcus, Sameer, Martha—how would you compare this list of existing success metrics to the candidate and hiring manager experiences we've sketched out?"

"I'm not seeing a lot of correlation," said Marcus, frowning. "Ultimately, a lot of these KPIs have nothing to do with what we want to happen. And some of them don't really make sense. Having fifteen candidates for every role exceeds

EXISTING
TALENT ACQUISITION KPIs

TIME To PoST	TIME To FILL
TIME To BUILD CANDIDATE PIPELINE	REJECTION RATE
CANDIDATE oPEN PoSITIoN RATIo	NEW EMPLOYEE RETENTIoN
CoST oF HIRING	CAMPUS HIRE SUCCESS RATE
% REQS oPEN VS. CLoSED	INTERNAL REFERRALS
	CoST PER HIRE

benchmarks, but maybe that's why it's taking our hiring managers so long to get through the process. There are just too many people to interview, especially if the fifteen are not the right people."

"And if Elke's team is under pressure to post jobs as quickly as possible," added Sameer, "then I can see how a recruiter might cut corners with a job description, especially if the system is hard to use. My team deals with conflicts like that all the time. We have a call time KPI that's part of our HR support center agents' performance evaluation. Their bonuses depend in part on keeping calls short, but sometimes an employee's issue is complex and the agent ends up rushing through an explanation; then our HRBPs get complaints, which always end up on my desk. I've always despised that

KPI because I saw that it drove the wrong behavior, but I could never convince anyone to change it."

"Great transition, Sameer," said Pam, "your concerns about KPIs are exactly what I want to discuss next." Pam moved to a new section of the whiteboard and took a new color marker from the wall-mounted whiteboard pen holder. "If we were more concerned with the effectiveness of the hiring process, versus the efficiency, what KPIs might we look at instead?"

Marcus leaned forward in his chair. "I've always thought our KPIs were out of whack! Like the rest of the business, we should be driving toward outcomes, starting with satisfaction ratings or Net Promoter Scores®. We have an NPS for Exalted customers, so why not our internal customers, in this case hiring managers? And why not for job candidates? Wouldn't that be a great shortcut to finding out whether we're delivering on expectations?"

Martha chimed in: "What if we introduced a more rigorous candidate quality metric? That's what hiring managers want, right? The right people for the job? If recruiters passed on fewer, better candidates to hiring managers, I don't see how we *wouldn't* cut time to hire."

"And that would bump up the acceptance rate, by giving candidates a more streamlined overall experience, no?" Sameer asked the group. The others nodded slowly but emphatically.

"It's probably too much to ask," added Martha, "but I've been asking forever that we require hiring managers to complete our course on behavioral interviewing. I'm sure that would contribute to hiring better candidates and increasing the acceptance rate. Studies show that behavioral interviews create a much better experience for everyone and lead to new hires staying longer and being more successful."

"Yes, behavioral interviewing should help along all the KPIs you've mentioned, Martha. I agree on making that part of every manager's development plan. Thank you, everyone. This is great thinking, and a solid start," declared Pam, moving aside to reveal the last list of the day.

OUTCOME-FOCUSED TALENT ACQUISITION KPIs

CANDIDATE NPS

HIRING MANAGER NPS

CANDIDATE QUALITY

OFFER ACCEPTANCE RATE

TIME TO HIRE

"Elke, I hope you feel you've gotten a head start. You know, you've been doing your job *as you were asked to do it*. But it's time that we modified our success criteria to drive toward business outcomes, not just cost efficiencies. I'd like each of you to review your own KPIs through this new lens, and together over the next few weeks we'll adjust them so that your incentives are aligned with where this company wants to go."

"That sounds great, Pam," said Sameer cautiously, "and I have a good idea about how to start the process based on today's brainstorming, but I might need some help."

"Great," Pam exclaimed. "I have someone for you to meet, but it's been a long morning, so first things first: lunch!"

As the team began to pack up, Marcus whispered to Elke, "If only Pam knew how little is expected of HR around here. I appreciate her optimism, but you know how hard it is to get our executives to change their ways. I just hope we're not setting ourselves up for disappointment."

"My thoughts exactly," Elke sighed.

SUMMARY

Pam takes her new leadership team to watch the Bulls play the Warriors. Running into her college basketball coach, she invites him along to the Exalted corporate box. There he shares his new data-driven approach to recruiting with Pam and an antagonistic Bobby Cash, Exalted CSO, who prefers his intuition to analytics. Pam remains friendly but firm about her team's direction. At the next day's off-site, the team explores ideal candidate and hiring manager experiences, using design thinking techniques; discussing Exalted Talent Acquisition metrics, however, they realize these key performance indicators (KPIs) don't track such results. Pam encourages them to pursue KPIs that measure effectiveness, not just efficiency. She tells the team she wants them to meet someone, but first they break for lunch.

COMMENTARY

FINDING AND BUILDING ALLIES

Pam and her new team have begun their journey to understanding business outcomes through data analytics, but there's a long way to go. One roadblock is Bobby Cash, who seems to resent both Pam and the very notion of data analytics. As his resistance demonstrates, moving to a data-driven leadership culture—like any change effort—will bring out the best in some people and the worst in others. Some will instantly grasp its meaning and potential, while people like Bobby are skeptical, cynical, or worse. It's important to find allies early, as detractors may be frequent and fervent.

Another reason to seek allies is practical. Most HR organizations lack the experience and clout to single-handedly lead a data analytics change effort across the corporation. Build strong relationships with leaders from one or more lines of business, such as sales, marketing, or operations, and you can gain:

- **Understanding:** These functions tend already to be engaged in data analytics and thus have familiarity and resources valuable to an analytically aspiring HR team.
- **Access:** Teams already heavily using analytics are likely data gatekeepers whose cooperation (and data) you will need to be successful, a topic highlighted in later chapters.
- **Advice:** Analytics-minded executives can help focus change efforts on concrete, measurable business outcomes, avoiding potentially narrower, HR-focused issues (recall Pam's early advice: think beyond HR to the entire company).

Pam and her team will need to win over Bobby and other leaders to successfully drive their analytics initiatives. Watch for this to unfold.

STEPPING INTO YOUR CUSTOMERS' SHOES

As Pam and team explore changing their thinking around measuring outcomes, she grounds the conversation in design thinking, a well-respected methodology developed at legendary Silicon Valley design firm IDEO and matured at the Hasso Plattner School of Design Thinking at Stanford University (see Figure 2c.1.).

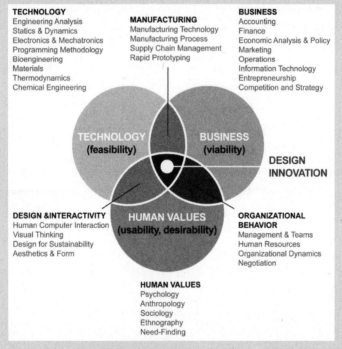

Figure 2c.1. Design Thinking

Source: DT Venn Diagram Created by the Author

The three foundational elements are grounded in empathy for the end-user:

1. Desirability/Usability: Will end-users want and need this solution?
2. Feasibility: What can reasonably be accomplished, technically and organizationally?
3. Viability: What is financially sustainable?

Pam steers her team toward hiring, a significant pain point for Exalted that is also highly transactional in nature, generating plenty of data that can be harnessed to understand impact. By asking them to define what candidates and hiring managers want, Pam leads her team to discover for themselves that they're measuring activity, not outcomes. These "rearview mirror KPIs" reflect what's happened, but not much more, and can even lead HR organizations in the wrong direction.

For example, Marcus realizes that having fifteen candidates for each role may exceed industry benchmarks, but it doesn't achieve their goal: to quickly find and hire the best person for the job. Elke is proud of their low cost to hire, saying they're "not throwing money at candidates like some of our competitors," yet they may be losing out on key talent by offering under-market compensation packages.

MOVING FROM ACTIVITY TO IMPACT

Let's look for a moment at rearview mirror KPIs in another area of HR. A classic example is training course completions (aka "butts in seats"). Many Learning & Development organizations—and their stakeholders—see completions as a success metric, although attendance has little bearing on learning outcomes. Similarly, many L&D professionals use learner evaluation scores as evidence of impact, yet our research shows that these survey results are typically driven by room temperature, food quality, and whether the presenter was entertaining.

Assessing whether the course achieved its defined goals and objectives requires an entirely different, and more sophisticated, set of questions and measures, but will enable learning teams to prove to their stakeholders—and themselves—that their efforts positively impacted the business. Yet as Pam points out, the VP of Talent Acquisition has been doing her job *as she was asked to do it*, just as L&D teams focused on attendance and learner evaluations are likely fulfilling the expectations of their internal customers. This brings us to an incredibly important point:

> ***We must take the initiative.*** HR professionals must not—indeed cannot—wait for business stakeholders to change their expectations of us. It is up to us to instead hold our executives accountable for defining desired business outcomes, and have them hold us accountable for tracking our impact on those outcomes.

This mindset change is the critical first step, not just toward measuring impact instead of activity but also toward evolving the expectations that we and our business owners have of each other.

A WORD ON LANGUAGE

The book that preceded this one, *Data Driven: How Performance Analytics Delivers Extraordinary Sales Results*, was filled with references to "big data." At the time of its publication in 2015, big data was everywhere. *The New York Times* declared "the Age of Big Data,"[1] while *Harvard Business Review* trumpeted a "management revolution"[2] fueled by big data. Data scientists, the mysterious practitioners of the analytics arts, were suddenly sexy.[3]

Big data can be explained simply as "the ability to process a large amount of complex information to make better-informed decisions."[4] The term more often used these days is *data analytics*, also called data science or business analytics, which is a scientific process that turns raw data (big or otherwise) into usable data.

Jeffrey Stanton, professor and senior associate dean in the School of Information Studies at Syracuse University, refers to data analytics as "an emerging area of work concerned with the collection, preparation, analysis, visualization, management, and preservation of large collections of information."[5]

The data language landscape is just one aspect of analytics that is constantly changing. To stay informed and reduce frustration, read up on major developments and don't be thrown by new terminology (or anything else new about analytics) that may appear.

THE TREND THAT STAYED

While "big data" appears less often in the business and mainstream media, the advances this phrase represents are hardly a passing fad. In fact, in January 2017, Ted Friedman, vice president and distinguished analyst at Gartner, cited three key trends in "data and analytics":[6]

- Data and analytics will not only reflect a company's performance, but will also drive business operations.
- Organizations will approach data and analytics holistically, using new end-to-end architectures.
- Senior leaders will integrate data and analytics into business strategy, generating new roles and opportunities to drive growth for data and analytics professionals.

Another indication that data analytics is here to stay is the increase in companies with a chief data officer, 54 percent of firms surveyed, according to a 2016 report, up from just 12 percent in 2012.[7] But we need look no further than our own pockets to understand that data analytics is practically ubiquitous. We all generate data whenever we carry a smartphone, use a credit card, open an app, stream services, buy something online, and myriad other daily activities. While data privacy, data security, and discrimination based on data are growing concerns, potential benefits from artificial intelligence and machine learning built on big data stretch from disease prevention to space exploration.[8]

And yet the Corporate Executive Board (CEB) found that HR professionals are not routinely using data to inform their people processes. Most companies do not monitor candidates or link candidate experiences to business objectives, and only about half use talent metrics to inform business decisions.[9]

It's time to catch up.

NOTES

1. Steve Lohr, "How Big Data Became So Big," *New York Times*, August 12, 2012, accessed May 25, 2017, http://www.nytimes .com/2012/08/12/business/how-big-data-became-so-big -unboxed.html?_r=0&pagewanted=print.

2. Andrew McAfee and Erik Brynjolfsson, "Big Data: The Management Revolution," *Harvard Business Review*, October 2012, accessed May 25, 2017, https://hbr.org/2012/10/big-data-the -management-revolution.

3. Thomas H. Davenport and D.J. Patil, "Data Scientist: The Sexiest Job of the 21st Century," *Harvard Business Review*, October 2012, accessed May 25, 2017, http://hbr.org/2012/10/ data-scientist-the-sexiest-job-of-the-21st-century/ar/pr.

4. Sanjeev Sardana and Sandeep Sardana, "Big Data: It's Not a Buzzword; It's a Movement," *Forbes*, last modified November 20, 2013, accessed May 25, 2017, https://www.forbes.com/ sites/sanjeevsardana/2013/11/20/bigdata/.

5. Jeffrey Stanton, *An Introduction to Data Science* (Syracuse, NY: n.p., 2013), ii, accessed May 25, 2017, https://archive.org/ details/DataScienceBookV3.

6. Rob van der Muelen, "2017: The Year That Data and Analytics Go Mainstream," Gartner, Inc., last modified January 24, 2017, accessed May 25, 2017, http://www.gartner.com/ smarterwithgartner/2017-the-year-that-data-and-analytics-go -mainstream/.

7. Randy Bean, "Big Data and the Emergence of the Chief Data Officer," *Forbes*, last modified August 8, 2016, accessed May 25, 2017, https://www.forbes.com/sites/ciocentral/2016/08/08/ big-data-and-the-emergence-of-the-chief-data-officer/print/.

8. Bernard Marr, "The Complete Beginner's Guide to Big Data in 2017," *Forbes*, last modified March 14, 2017, accessed May 25,

2017, https://www.forbes.com/sites/bernardmarr/2017/03/14/the-complete-beginners-guide-to-big-data-in-2017/print/.

9. Tracy M. Kantrowitz, *Global Assessment Trends 2014* (London: CEB Global, 2015), accessed May 25, 2017, https://www.cebglobal.com/content/dam/cebglobal/us/EN/regions/uk/tm/pdfs/Report/gatr-2014.pdf.

Chapter 3

STARTING WITH ANALYTICS

The team had filed back into the conference room after lunch and settled into their seats when Pam walked in with a young woman and a large box of chocolate truffles from a well-known local purveyor.

"Chicago's finest!" Pam declared, motioning first toward the guest and then the chocolates. "I've brought with me two very important components for the final portion of our off-site. The first will help keep our energy up and our imaginations going. I've been somewhat obsessed with this brand ever since I stopped by their kiosk at O'Hare."

"I love that chocolate," exclaimed Sameer. "Pam, you have my attention now."

"I wish I'd known how easy it could be, Sameer," said Pam with a smile, handing him the box. Sameer excitedly picked one out and then passed them around. Pam then turned back to the group. "Second, and most important, is Chloe Curtis, the person I mentioned I wanted you all to meet. Chloe is a data scientist. She'll help us navigate our analytics challenges on a project basis for the next few months, and I'm excited to have her on board."

"Chloe is top-notch," said Pam. "She earned a prestigious master of science in analytics from the McCormick School of Engineering at Northwestern and a double undergraduate degree from Stanford in statistics and psychology, which she felt were a good complement to her interest in HR. She completed *two* grad school internships in corporate HR departments and was hired by a top HR consulting firm into their analytics practice, where she worked on some pretty advanced projects, including developing a candidate scoring app. Now she's independent, and she came highly recommended from a former colleague of mine who watched her meteoric rise at the consulting firm."

The team was duly impressed.

"I was able to attract her to Exalted," Pam explained, "because of the unique opportunity to get to the bottom of some serious corporate challenges. She wants to get three to four years of independent experience and then earn her Ph.D. in machine learning. And it didn't hurt that she's from Berkeley and we are united as members of Dub Nation," she concluded, with a knowing smile to Chloe.

Pam then introduced each of the team members, sharing their credentials with Chloe and praising their capabilities. Marcus, Martha, Elke, and Sameer couldn't help but be impressed with the time she'd taken to learn their backgrounds. Pam continued, "At Trajectory, we were successful using analytics to revive sales enablement because we brought in an outside expert who had fresh eyes and knew how to ask the right questions, find the right data, and ultimately identify the answers. Chloe will help us to do that here."

"Sounds good to me," said Marcus, "but where do we start? I don't mind admitting that I could use some basic information about analytics."

"You guys are all about the perfect segues today," Pam declared. "That's next. Chloe, why don't you get set up while we dig into the chocolates."

Chloe pulled an enormous laptop out of her bag and Elke helped her plug into the projector. "How do you lug that thing around? It must weigh a ton," Martha marveled.

From Chloe's bemused look, it was clear that her laptop elicited that response often. "Yeah, serious analytics work requires more computing power than people realize," she replied. "Consider that your first piece of analytics trivia. Now let's start with some fundamentals." She presented her first slide.

"This is a general framework for how to think about using data to address business challenges," Chloe began, "It's the four stages of analytics. It's not the only way to think about analytics, but it's a good one, and I find that it makes sense to most people, especially if you're new to the field.

"The four stages, or types, of analytics are progressively more complex, and, generally speaking, each successive stage produces more valuable output," Chloe continued. "The first stage is *descriptive analytics*, which essentially answers the question, 'What's happened?' Most basic reports and dashboards display descriptive analytics."

"I'm already more familiar with those than I'd like to be," Sameer said wryly. "Some days I feel like all my team does is crank out reports."

"I'd love to look at those, Sameer," said Chloe. "Pam told me you hold most of the responsibility for HR reporting, so we will definitely be spending some time together. We'll figure out how to gain more insights from the data you

Four Stages of Analytics

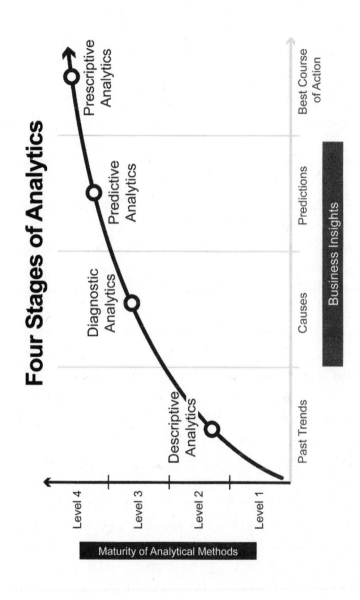

have, and then let's hope that running reports will feel like a rewarding, creative task instead of a pointless chore."

"First truffles, and now this. A banner day!" Sameer exclaimed, making the others chuckle.

"Happy to be of service," said Pam with a nod. "Go on, Chloe."

"So, after you figure out what happened, the next natural question is 'Why?' 'Why' is the most important word in analytics. We dig deeper until we get to the root cause. In the second stage of analytics, *diagnostic analytics*, we look for the 'why' by identifying relationships among data, using various statistical and analytical techniques."

"Our internal clients would be thrilled to know why things have gone so wrong for us," said Marcus. "I just hope most of the blame doesn't land on our desks."

"I can't make any promises there," smiled Chloe. "It's easy to point fingers at HR, but in my experience, a lot of what goes wrong is caused by a combination of misunderstandings, missed clues, outdated technology, and straight up human denial, often on the part of the business owners. And while getting people to *accept* what the data says is a topic for another day, what's great about analytics is that data may prove that HR isn't to blame."

"Wouldn't *that* be amazing?" Martha wondered aloud.

Chloe nodded and continued. "The third stage builds on the second one. Once we know why something is happening, we can use data to figure out what could happen next— that's *predictive analytics*. This is when we'd start using tools like modeling and machine learning. Finally, once you have a sense of what's going to happen next, you can plan for it in the fourth stage using *prescriptive analytics*, which explores a set of possibilities and suggests optimal courses of action."

Chloe walked over to a whiteboard and began to write. "I know that's a lot of information to take in. I think it will make more sense as we dive into some analytics and see it in action. Meanwhile, here's a summary chart to keep in mind."

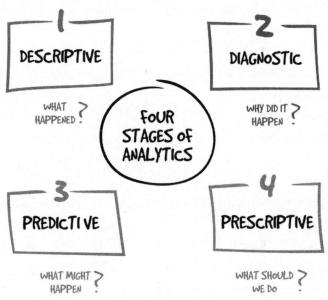

"Thanks, Chloe," said Pam. "This is a great foundation for understanding our data analytics initiatives. I suggest we start to put theory into practice with Sales, and not just because Bobby is our most vocal stakeholder. His results are most closely tied to revenue and, at least in his mind, his issues link directly to HR."

"When I had lunch with him last week, Bobby laid out the issues," Pam continued. "According to him, he doesn't have enough sales reps who can hit quota. He's losing his top producers,* and can't find enough good reps to hire to replace them. He says he can't onboard fast enough the reps he does find, so managers pitch in with sales, meaning they don't have time to interview candidates or bring new reps up to speed."

"Pass the truffles. Martha and I are going to need them," said Elke with a dejected sigh.

"Come on now," Pam said, "Don't despair. Let me show you something. I know from previous data analytics projects that it's critical to brainstorm all the potential factors at work—the pieces of the puzzle. At Trajectory, we wanted to understand sales rep performance, so our first step was to come up with all the key performance indicators that impact bookings.

"I was feeling nostalgic," she said, plugging the HDMI cable back into her own laptop and projecting a slide onto the screen, "so here's the photo I took of the KPI 'tree' we created in a marathon brainstorming session to identify all the different branches of impact."

---

*In this book, a "producer" generates revenue while a "performer" meets or exceeds his or her sales goals (called quota). So a "top producer" would have higher sales than most other reps, while a "top performer" would also meet or exceed quota. Reps who are top producers but do not make quota are not top performers. You'll find out more in Chapter 5.

TOTAL SALES REP BOOKINGS

OF OPPORTUNITIES IN PIPELINE

 # OF TARGET ACCOUNTS
- # OF TARGET GEOGRAPHIES
- # OF TARGET INDUSTRIES

 # OF LEADS GENERATED
- # OF MARKETING CAMPAIGNS
- # OF CHANNELS

LEAD CONVERSION RATE
- LEAD FOLLOW-UP RATE
- LEAD QUALITY SCORE

AVERAGE DEAL SIZE

 # OF PRODUCTS /DEAL (BUNDLING)
- # OF UNIQUE PRODUCTS IN PIPELINE PER REP
- % OF BUNDLED PRODUCT DEALS

 # OF UNITS SOLD/DEAL
- % OF PIPELINE OPPORTUNITIES W/ LARGE ACCOUNTS
- AVERAGE CONTRACT LENGTH

AVERAGE SELLING PRICE/UNIT
- AVERAGE DISCOUNT RATE
- % OF PIPELINE FOCUSED ON HIGH VALUE PRODUCTS

WIN RATE

% OF UPSELL DEALS
- NET PROMOTER SCORE
- % OF UPSELL DEALS

% OF ABANDONED DEALS
- % OF HIGH PROBABILITY DEALS
- AVERAGE # DAYS PER SALES STAGE

SALES SUPPORT COVERAGE RATIO
- MANDATORY SALES TRAINING COMPLIANCE
- PRESALES SUPPORT COVERAGE

"From there, our data consultant—a real character named Henry Crawford—pulled data from different parts of the business and defined *137 variables* impacting sales rep performance," Pam continued, advancing to a new slide.

Sales Rep/KPI Performance Analysis
Data Sources

"Henry was then able to determine which variables most impact rep attainment, and rank them in order of influence. Ultimately, he used that data to develop what he called 'ideal sales rep DNA,' which we used to guide training, coaching, and, of course, hiring. There's a lot more to the story—for now I'll just say that I'm giving this data to Chloe to significantly shorten our project time here," Pam concluded.

"But will this 'DNA' be the same for Exalted as it was for Trajectory?" asked Sameer.

"It's unlikely, but it provides a tremendous shortcut," answered Chloe. "Success criteria vary from one company to the next, but leveraging the process Pam's consultant used to uncover that DNA will save me a lot of time. I've already taken a look, and I'm confident I can use a similar approach to determine the Exalted sales rep DNA without a lot of effort."

"First, though, we need to brainstorm the factors at work here at Exalted," Pam declared, "and start to understand what might be causing sales reps to leave."

"Absolutely," said Chloe. "With descriptive analytics, we first determine what to measure, depending on what variables matter for the outcomes you are interested in. Some might be key performance indicators, some might be other metrics, and some might not fit neatly into any category. I'll just refer to all of them as KPIs for short. So our first step is to identify KPIs. I'll start a list."

Chloe wrote on the nearest whiteboard: "Initial Steps" and then underneath it began a numbered list, starting with, "Identify KPIs."

"Let's start with the top-level influencers of reps leaving," Pam suggested. "Chloe, will you take notes please?" Chloe nodded, labeling a new list "Sales Rep Attrition."

"Obviously, engagement is going to be a top factor," Martha stated. "They won't stick around if they're not happy here."

"That's true," said Pam, seeing that others were poised to jump in, "but I'm going to challenge us to first think about the business angle and then get to the HR angle. Are you all game?"

The team nodded somewhat reluctantly, seeing that Pam would keep her promise of trying to change their mindset but not feeling quite sure what that would require.

Marcus dove in. "I've been working with Bobby long enough to know that the top attrition driver for salespeople is whether they're making money."

"That's right, Marcus," said Pam. "And making money is tied to 'attainment,' or how much revenue the rep is bringing in. Speaking more generally, we could boil that down to 'employee performance.'"

Chloe began to write:

"Now, what are the drivers of rep attainment?" asked Pam.

Martha raised her hand and said, "I've got this one. I used to be an instructional designer for sales training. There are multiple factors, but the most important is quota, because a rep's commissions depend on whether she or he makes quota. And despite what Bobby says, I think the second most important factor is a rep's development. I wish I had a dollar for every sales manager who thinks that a newly hired experienced rep doesn't need training on our products," she said, sighing.

"Speaking of managers," Elke chimed in, "I think they need their own training. I've noticed that a lot of the hiring managers who drag their feet on selecting candidates are the same ones who keep showing up with open positions because their reps leave. They seem pretty clueless when it comes to the people manager part of their jobs."

"Elke, good to know I'm not the only one seeing the negative repercussions of managers skipping out on leadership development courses," said Martha, looking relieved and suddenly hopeful. "I practically begged Bobby to make some of these courses mandatory, but he wouldn't budge. 'My managers are *wayyyy* too important to waste time sitting around in a classroom,'" she said, imitating Bobby's Louisiana drawl.

Pam couldn't help but grin. "Looks like we'll have plenty of opportunities to enhance our impact," she said enthusiastically. "What else?"

"Well," began Sameer, "I recently met the field marketing manager at an internal IT task force. We hit it off and had lunch together. I learned that qualifying and passing leads to sales reps is very important. But this manager seemed to have as many complaints as I do about the need for systems upgrades to make sure reps receive the right leads."

"You guys know an impressive amount about sales and what could go wrong with sales," Pam said with a nod. "What other factors come into play?"

"Something else I hear a lot from Bobby is that reps who can't sell will try to deflect blame by claiming that our prices are too high," added Marcus. "So even if it's an excuse, it seems logical that pricing would impact a rep's ability to sell."

"So would our products," Sameer declared. "That field marketing manager told me in confidence that her team says they have trouble generating new leads because companies want lower-cost solutions and not our premier offerings. But when she mentioned it at a sales leadership team meeting, everyone said it couldn't be true, especially Bobby. True or not, I would think that offering the right products would be fundamental to sales success."

"This is exactly the kind of business thinking we need," Pam exclaimed, motioning to the notes Chloe had taken on the whiteboard.

"Now let's get back to our comfort zone," Pam said. "What are the factors impacting a rep's engagement level?"

Martha was the first speak up. "The number one reason most people leave a company is their manager. Given that sales managers tend to skip out on leadership development courses, and according to Elke aren't great at hiring or keeping people, I would say that's a major culprit."

"I'd agree—manager issues are definitely a big factor," said Marcus. "Three other things impact sales rep engagement. First, as I mentioned before, can they make money? Second, is their sales territory viable? That's kind of a proxy for how they feel they're treated. If their territory is industry-based and requires a ton of travel, that can make them feel put-upon. A small territory can make them feel they've been set up for failure. All that can cause resentment and erode engagement."

"All true," nodded Pam.

"Great. And third," Marcus continued, "do they believe in their company's products—at least enough to sell them? It's hard to imagine that's a factor at Exalted though. We've been the premium provider in the market for as long as I've worked here, and that's nearly twenty years."

"Wouldn't annual employee engagement survey scores be a pretty obvious indicator?" asked Elke.

"They would indeed," Pam replied.

Chloe finished adding "engagement scores" to the growing list and turned to face the group. "Building on what Marcus just said, another top-level attrition factor for our list is the employer brand. It really influences employees' fundamental attitudes. In one of my HR consulting projects, we determined that two major scandals contributed to a 5 percent increase in annual turnover. People just didn't want to work there anymore. The company also had a hard time attracting job candidates."

"That would confirm your sinking ship analysis, Marcus," said Sameer, adding, "I thought the same thing."

"Elke, how are we currently tracking our employer brand?" Pam asked.

"Our employer brand . . . ?" Elke responded quizzically. "Exalted has always been the market leader so we've never thought about measuring the employer brand. I think we'd look at things like number of employee referrals and number of applicants per posted job. Those weren't great in the latest report, but I think most companies are experiencing a drop around now."

"Great that we are generating reports on those KPIs," said Pam, "but having data isn't the same as understanding that data. Chloe, could we do some trend analysis or correlation analysis to understand what's happening with employee referrals and applicant numbers?"

"Sure," Chloe answered. "What about external data? Do you track comments on social media, perhaps on your company's Facebook page, LinkedIn, or Glassdoor?"

"We don't track that in any concerted way," answered Elke. "That seems like a lot of work."

"Actually," Chloe explained, "these days it's possible to use web crawlers to aggregate data and extract any comments about a given company, then do sentiment analysis to determine whether the comments are positive or negative."

"I'd love to know what's being said about Exalted all over the Internet," Elke's voice raised in excitement. "I wish I'd known sooner how easy it would be to do."

"We might also consider applying for employer awards, like the '100 Best Places to Work,'" Pam commented. "That's another way to learn about—and perhaps promote—our employer brand. But I know we're on Glassdoor, so that's good for now."

"Great," said Chloe, finishing the KPI "tree" and stepping back to give everyone a look.

"Seems like I've got some work to do. Anything else to add here for now?" Chloe asked, looking around the room.

"Seems like a solid starting point to me," said Pam.

"Great," said Chloe, turning to an empty stretch of whiteboard. "Now let's talk about what kind of data sources will help us. That discussion will be both useful to me and I hope instructive to you as you build your understanding of HR analytics." She continued, drawing a four-cell matrix. "Let me show you a framework and we can fill it in together."

DATA TO COLLECT ON SALES REP ATTRITION

	STRUCTURED	UNSTRUCTURED
INTERNAL		
EXTERNAL		

"These are the different types of data we'll be collecting," Chloe explained. "To greatly oversimplify, stuff we can quantify is structured, and stuff we can't quantify is unstructured. For example, I'm sure Sameer can track calls to your call center. Data like call length and number of rings before a call was answered would be structured data—pretty straightforward to measure and analyze. Audio recordings of calls would be unstructured data. They'll have plenty of useful information, but we'll have to work harder to extract it."

Elke broke in, "Let me see whether I've got this right. How long it takes the average user to upload a résumé is structured data, but comments about the process of uploading résumés on Glassdoor would be unstructured?"

"Yup," Chloe answered. "And the résumé upload data is internal, while the Glassdoor reviews are external."

The team brainstormed until they had entered all the KPIs from the tree into the data collection matrix. "This is a great start," Chloe declared, stepping aside from the whiteboard so the team could see their progress.

"So now that we know what we're looking for," said Chloe, returning to the list she'd started earlier, "the next step in the process is getting our hands on the data. We have to find it and then collect it." She wrote "Locate and collect data" on the whiteboard.

"How do we gain access to the data?" asked Marcus.

"I'll make sure the right people know they need to prioritize sharing data," answered Pam. "David will back me up if needed. I know from experience that this can be an issue for all kinds of reasons. Some people are very territorial about their data, the same way they're territorial about anything else; some are concerned about confidentiality, others are nervous—with or without reason—that it could expose unflattering issues within their organization. But this is a business problem, and the business should want to play ball.

DATA TO COLLECT ON SALES REP ATTRITION

	STRUCTURED	UNSTRUCTURED
INTERNAL	- QUOTA – DIFF BETWEEN QUOTA POTENTIAL AND TERRITORY ASSIGNED - STRATEGIC TRAINING COVERAGE RATIO – % OF TRAINING RESOURCES COVERING TOP REVENUE DRIVERS - MARKETING QUALIFIED LEADS (MQL) – # LEADS PASSED TO REPS - COMP (BASE + COMMISSIONS) - MANAGER RATINGS – INDIVIDUAL: 360 REVIEWS - MANAGER RATINGS – AGGREGATE: ENGAGEMENT SURVEY SCORES - # REFERRALS (ABSOLUTE # USED IN CONVERSION RATIO; LARGER ACCOUNTS MEAN FEWER REFERRALS NEEDED) - # JOB APPLICANTS PER POST	- QUALITATIVE ENGAGEMENT SURVEY FEEDBACK
EXTERNAL	- EMPLOYER RANKING, E.G. GLASSDOOR - PRICE – DIFFERENCE BETWEEN OUR PRODUCT'S PRICE AND THE MEDIAN PRICE OF ALL COMPETITIVE PRODUCTS - SALES OF ORGANIC VS. ACQUIRED VS. EXTERNAL PRODUCTS	- GLASSDOOR, OTHER SOCIAL MEDIA COMMENTS

Marcus, thank you in advance for having your HRBPs work with their clients to support our efforts. It sounds like you'd be more than willing to help Chloe with business context and insights."

"Absolutely," Marcus agreed.

"Thanks, Marcus," responded Chloe. "Data analysts always need people who know the business to help make sense of the data and put things in context."

"I'm sure you can count on the rest of the team for insights as well. Right?" Pam asked, looking around the room.

"Right!"

"Even with all your help, which I definitely appreciate, I just want to warn everyone," cautioned Chloe, "that hunting down data can be frustrating. Many times, the data will be poor quality or simply incorrect, systems won't talk to each other, data will get lost—issues like that."

Sameer nodded vigorously. "I wish I didn't know so much about this subject! I can relate to data frustrations. So, Chloe, if you have data questions, I'll be your point person. Come to me any time. I may even be able to spare some of my analysts to help you with the heavy lifting."

"That's great, Sameer," Chloe responded with enthusiasm, then got serious again. "Once we have access to the data, we'll have to pull it, and then we'll have to clean it up so it's usable. Cleaning data is about as fun as it sounds—removing empty fields or incorrectly entered data that can mess up analytical models. We could run into a variety of other issues, but let's leave it at that for now."

69

"Once we have a clean data set, I'll take a close look at what we've collected," continued Chloe. "To start making sense of our data, I'll spend some time plotting variables against each other."

"OK, I feel like the tech-speak police, but could you explain 'plotting variables'?" asked Martha, looking perplexed again.

"Oops. Sorry, Martha. Stop me any time with questions," Chloe replied. "As I mentioned earlier, 'variable' is another term for KPI. By plotting variables against each other, I mean visually charting how different KPIs interact. For example, I might look at employee engagement versus employee performance, to see whether engagement goes up as performance goes up. It's fairly basic analysis, but it can identify patterns, trends, and problem areas."

Chloe added the most recent details to the list, so the whiteboard now read:

INITIAL STEPS

1) IDENTIFY KPIS

2) LOCATE AND COLLECT DATA

- IDENTIFY SOURCES (DATABASES) OF KPIS (VARIABLES)

- GAIN ACCESS TO DATABASES

- PULL DATA

- CLEAN DATA

3) ANALYZE DATA AND IDENTIFY ISSUES (DESCRIPTIVE ANALYTICS)

Pam congratulated the team on a highly productive afternoon and adjourned the meeting. She was pleased with their progress, Chloe's initial success, and the apparent disappearance of the previous day's "Blame Game" tensions.

She wondered, though, what challenges lay ahead as data requests started to circulate. She knew that analytics initiatives could be stymied or derailed completely by powerful leaders unwilling to hand over their data, especially to someone new. She had confidence in David, but she hadn't been at Exalted long enough to know who might sabotage their efforts before they had a chance to prove their worth.

"Is everything all right, Pam?" asked Marcus, reading her expression as the team packed up for the day.

"Absolutely," Pam answered with a broad smile, holding the conference room door open as the group filed out.

SUMMARY

At the last segment of their off-site, Pam introduced data analytics consultant Chloe Curtis, a young but experienced data scientist who would be helping the team unravel what was going wrong at Exalted Enterprises.

Chloe familiarizes the team with the four stages of analytics, structured and unstructured data, and the overall analytics process. Pam tells the team she's given Chloe a head start by sharing some of the analytics work done at her previous company, which began with identifying relevant KPIs and led to determining the "ideal sales rep DNA." The team then brainstorms KPIs impacting sales rep attrition, identifying as three key realms: rep attraction, attainment, and satisfaction. They also identify data to seek out in these realms and agree to support Chloe as she tackles descriptive analytics.

COMMENTARY

INITIAL UNDERSTANDING

While it's important to grasp the fundamentals of data analytics, most HR experts will do well to hire one or more data analysts for the heavy lifting. As Clayton Christensen advises in his groundbreaking book *The Innovator's Dilemma*,[1] you just don't know what you don't know.

Even though Pam has considerable experience with analytics, she knows her limits and brings in an expert. Pam is confident that Chloe will be able to use her specialized expertise in people analytics to focus quickly on outcomes for Exalted, in partnership with Pam and her Human Resources leadership team. While not every organization can afford a full-time analytics person, it's important to have someone with technical expertise, even as a part-time consultant.

Pam and Chloe take time to ensure the team members understand the four stages of analytics to give them context, vocabulary, and fundamental knowledge. Although they are familiar with reports—even fancy ones that use data visualizations to show turnover trends, hiring statistics, or training attendance metrics—reports only represent basic descriptive analytics.

Organizations must take these first-level insights and then go deeper to understand the "why" behind them to gain insights into performance metrics such as productivity, profitability, customer satisfaction, and others. This is the heart of diagnostic, predictive, and prescriptive analytics (more on this below).

Chloe provides a simple but effective set of steps to follow. These can be a great way to begin your own project. Most importantly, be bold and fearless as you begin your journey toward a data driven leadership culture.

FAMILIARITY IS PARAMOUNT

Information without interpretation has little value. Similarly, analytics requires business understanding to give it meaning and power. It's relatively easy these days to "buy" the services of a data statistician. What you can't buy is someone who knows your organization and can ask the right questions.

The best partner for a data scientist is both knowledgeable about the business and relentlessly curious about what makes it tick. This type of person knows how to probe for understanding and judge whether data "feels right." Deep knowledge of your company, combined with data analytics prowess, is a winning combination.

THE FOUR STAGES OF ANALYTICS

As shown on the chart in the chapter and below (Figure 3c.1), data analytics is commonly categorized as descriptive, diagnostic, predictive, or prescriptive.

1. *Descriptive analytics* asks, "What has happened?" By mining data to provide trending information on past or current events, it provides decision-making guidance for future actions, often in the form of key performance indicators. Descriptive analytics data is usually displayed within reports or dashboards, which are sometimes automated to issue alerts or trigger actions at various thresholds. In day-to-day business operations, much of analytics is descriptive in nature.

2. *Diagnostic analytics* asks, "Why has this happened?" By utilizing statistical and analytical techniques to identify relationships in data sets and degrees of correlation between variables, it helps pinpoint the causes of problems and formulate corrective solutions. Exalted will begin using diagnostic analytics in Chapter 4, with the bulk of diagnostic analytics happening in Chapter 5.

3. *Predictive analytics* asks, "What could happen?" The term encompasses a variety of techniques, such as statistics, modeling, machine learning, and data mining, which are used for finding correlations within big sets of current and historical facts, to make useful predictions about future events. Predictive analytics appear in Chapter 6.

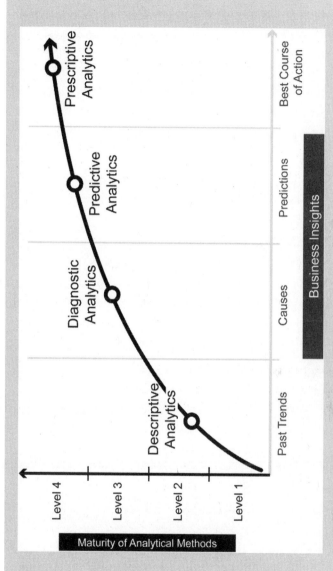

Figure 3c.1. The Four Stages of Analytics

4. *Prescriptive analytics* asks, "What should we do?" It explores a set of possibilities and suggests optimal course(s) of action based on descriptive and predictive analyses of complex data. Utilizing advanced analytical and mathematical models, it can also provide reasons for recommendations and possible implications of following them. We'll talk about this level of analytics in Chapter 6.

Additional insights on the four levels of analytics appear in *Essential Reading*, at the end of this book.

PEOPLE ANALYTICS TODAY

Where are most companies today vis-à-vis people analytics? The Bersin Talent Analytics Maturity Model outlines four levels or stages that organizations achieve as they hone their analytics capabilities, which are similar, yet not identical, to the four types listed above:

1. **Operational Reporting.** About half of all organizations use this level of reporting,[2] which is *reactive* and *descriptive*. Organizations at this level generally lack dedicated data analytics staff, and the focus tends to be on data accuracy, consistency, and timeliness in delivery. Most only measure two talent metrics: time-to-fill and diversity.[3]

2. **Advanced Reporting.** Some 30 percent of organizations use this reporting, likely to be *proactive* and *diagnostic*, aimed at understanding stakeholders' needs and

the metrics required to support their decision-making functions. Metrics may include measures of high-performance turnover, rate of employee promotion, cost-per-hire, effectiveness of recruiting, and quality of hire.[4] With dedicated staff, the analytics team helps leaders understand the numbers and how to act upon them.

3. **Advanced Analytics.** Just 10 percent of organizations use reporting that is strategic,[5] focused on understanding the root causes of organizational challenges to proactively *identify issues* and *recommend solutions*. Many organizations centralize their analytics teams at this stage, expanding metrics collection and sophistication of data analysis.

4. **Predictive Analytics.** Only 4 percent of organizations utilize predictive models[6] and scenario planning to "tell a story" easy for others to grasp, helping reduce and mitigate risk and integrate fully with organizational strategic planning and corporate development.

A 2015 IBM/HR.com poll yielded similar findings.[7] Although a little over half of respondents felt their organizations had clearly linked their business and talent strategies, only about one in ten (11 percent) were using prescriptive (3 percent) or predictive (8 percent) analytics, while most remained using basic reporting (41 percent) or descriptive analytics (48 percent).

Deloitte's *Global Human Capital Trends 2017* has good news and bad news about the field of analytics within Human Resources.[8]

- *The good news:* People analytics—the use of data analytics and digital tools to measure, report, and understand employee performance—has "gone mainstream," with 76 percent of U.S. companies terming it a high priority.[9] The report makes an apt observation: "Just as spreadsheets were once a tool of finance alone but are now used throughout business, people analytics is making a similar leap."
  - The top area of focus for people analytics are recruiting, performance measurement, compensation, workforce planning, and retention, with significant growth in companies using organizational network analysis (ONA) and interaction analytics (studying employee behavior) to identify and understand business enhancement opportunities.
  - About half of HR leaders are restructuring their offerings to leverage digital and mobile tools, while a third have adopted some form of artificial intelligence (AI) in their delivery of HR services.[10]
  - HR is supporting organizational culture shifts to achieve these analytics goals, and it is also now expected to take a leading role in the digital transformation of organizations, spearheading the drive to redesign how business is done in the digital age.
- *The bad news:* Just 8 percent of organizations say they have usable data, while less than 10 percent believe they understand which dimensions of talent are performance drivers.[11]

So, although there has been plenty of progress, there's still far to go. *Don't wait.*

OTHER ROADBLOCKS

A 2014 survey of 230 business executives, HR professionals, and managers reported that the key roadblocks to realizing better use of data analytics for HR are:

- **Institutional constraints:** inaccurate, inconsistent, or hard-to-access data (54 percent); lack of HR analytics skills/training (47 percent); and lack of adequate investment in resources (44 percent).
- **Cultural constraints:** leaders and employees do not see value in a data driven culture (37 percent); lack of C-suite support (29 percent); and HR does not know how to successfully relate analytics to business outcomes (27 percent).[12]

Some of these findings are echoed in a 2015 article in *McKinsey Quarterly*, which notes three factors that can bog down data analytics efforts:[13]

1. Senior decision-makers may balk at investing in analytics, often because initial forays into analytics yielded modest results. These may have been at the dawn of the "big data" era, when enthusiasm may have outweighed experience in turning data into transformative insights.
2. Decision-makers often lack confidence that analytics will improve their decision making, in part because analytics tools and processes are difficult to use or understand. They instead rely on old instincts or guidelines.
3. Existing corporate practices may frustrate the collection and analysis of data. Other than companies like

Facebook or Amazon, which have analytics at the core of their operations and mentality, it's a challenge to integrate data into the corporate infrastructure and decision-making processes.

What's holding your organization back? This is a sincere question to carefully consider. In the Chapter 7 commentary, we'll share some guidelines on moving forward with your efforts, but for now it's important to begin cataloguing what might stand in the way of your success.

DATA ANALYTICS FYI: DATA CARE AND FEEDING

As Chloe mentioned, there are several steps between identifying your KPIs and getting down to the actual analysis. Two key steps will be handled by your data professionals, but it's good information for you to have to better understand both their process and what could hold it up.

1. *Assembling the KPIs:* Your data team will have to find out what data "fields" are available in the databases and how to combine them. For example, if your KPI of interest is "top performer retention," you'll need to pull in HR data such as "tenure," "performance ratings," "goals achieved," and more. Also, you may need convoluted algebra to combine five fields into a single KPI. Data from various sources are then merged into a single data set.
2. *Cleaning the data:* The freshly merged data set must then be cleaned. Any incomplete data must be filled in or removed. Similarly, any outlier—a number suspiciously larger or smaller than others within the same KPI—must

be removed. The data may also have to be scaled: If one of the variables ranges from 0 to 100, while another variable ranges from −1 to 1, many models will misinterpret the first variable as being 100 times more important than the second, although that is not necessarily true.

Other types of data cleaning and standardizations are too numerous to list here. It is important to note that improperly handled data can lead to erroneous conclusions and misplaced confidence, leading to faulty actions. Don't skimp on this phase. It sometimes requires more time to understand, locate, acquire, and clean data than to build the analytical model.

NOTES

1. Clayton N. Christensen, *The Innovator's Dilemma: The Revolutionary Book That Will Change the Way You Do Business* (New York: HarperBusiness, 1997/2011).
2. Josh Bersin, Karen O'Leonard, and Wendy Wang-Audia, *High-Impact Talent Analytics: Building a World-Class HR Measurement and Analytics Function* (Oakland, CA: Bersin & Associates, October 2013), 28, accessed May 25, 2017, http://www.bersin.com/Lib/Rs/ShowDocument.aspx?docid=16909.
3. Bersin, O'Leonard, and Wang-Audia, *High-Impact Talent Analytics*, 35.
4. Bersin, O'Leonard, and Wang-Audia, *High-Impact Talent Analytics*, 41, 44.
5. Bersin, O'Leonard, and Wang-Audia, *High-Impact Talent Analytics*, 57.
6. Bersin, O'Leonard, and Wang-Audia, *High-Impact Talent Analytics,* 72.

7. Leo F. Brajkovich and Victor J. Reyes, "Using Workforce Analytics to Deliver Your Business Strategy," HR.com, last modified November 18, 2015, accessed May 25, 2017, https://www.hr.com/en?t=/network/event/attachment .supply&fileID=1447773089804.

8. Bill Pelster and Jeff Schwartz (eds.), *Global Human Capital Trends 2017* (Westlake, TX: Deloitte UP, March 2017), accessed May 25, 2017, https://dupress.deloitte.com/dup-us-en/focus/ human-capital-trends.html.

9. Laurence Collins, Dave Fineman, and Akio Tsuchida, "People Analytics: Recalculating the Route," in *Global Human Capital Trends 2017*, Bill Pelster and Jeff Schwartz (eds.) (Westlake, TX: Deloitte UP, March 2017), 98, accessed May 25, 2017, https://dupress .deloitte.com/dup-us-en/focus/human-capital-trends.html.

10. Erica Volini, Pascal Occean, Michael Stephan, and Brett Walsh, "Digital HR: Platforms, People, Work," in *Global Human Capital Trends 2017*, Bill Pelster and Jeff Schwartz (eds.) (Westlake, TX: Deloitte UP, March 2017), 87, accessed May 25, 2017, https:// dupress.deloitte.com/dup-us-en/focus/human-capital-trends.html.

11. Collins, Fineman, and Tsuchida, "People Analytics," 97.

12. Harvard Business Review Analytics Services, *HR Joins the Analytics Revolution* (Brighton, MA: Harvard Business Publishing, July 2014), 6, accessed May 25, 2017, https://hbr.org/resources/ pdfs/comm/visier/18765_HBR_Visier_Report_July2014.pdf.

13. David Court, "Getting Big Impact from Big Data," *McKinsey Quarterly*, January 2015, accessed May 25, 2017, http://www.mckinsey .com/business-functions/digital-mckinsey/our-insights/getting -big-impact-from-big-data.

Chapter 4

EARLY DISCOVERIES

ONE WEEK POST OFF-SITE: FEBRUARY 18

In the week following the team off-site, as Marcus and Chloe began requesting data access from Exalted leaders, Pam's early concerns regarding peer reactions were confirmed. While David had backed her up as expected, she still ended up in conversations with peers suspicious about why she needed the data, what she planned to do with it, and in what timeframe.

Pam chose to view these conversations as opportunities to deepen relationships and establish trust, always through partnering and never confronting, so she was in good spirits as she headed down the hallway for an 11 a.m. meeting about the data initiative with the chief marketing officer, Anne Rodriguez.

"Anne, great to see you again," Pam said, entering Anne's office and striding over to shake her outstretched hand. They'd had good rapport at their breakfast meeting just after Pam started at Exalted, but there was a definite tension in the air.

"Thanks for taking time to chat about your data project," said Anne, removing her stylish red reading glasses as she took a seat across from Pam at the small meeting table in her office. "I wasn't quite sure I read the email request from Marcus and your consultant correctly."

"Yes, it's a new frontier for Exalted, but I've seen how essential analytics can be to turnarounds elsewhere," Pam agreed with enthusiasm. "As you know from our initial leadership team meeting with David, he sees potential for Exalted to get back on track by using data to understand and solve our business challenges. Of course, that requires all of us to share and interpret data in new ways."

"But surely you don't need all our raw data. Can't we just run the reports you need?" Anne asked, leaning forward in her chair. "I mean, flat files with the filters turned off? No one has ever asked for *that* before."

"Anne, I know that seems foreign for Exalted, but this kind of request is typical in companies that rely on analytics to drive their decision making," Pam reassured her. "Tell me what your concerns are."

Anne hesitated, then continued. "Honestly, I have a few concerns. The first is about protecting this company. We have strict rules governing how we use customer data, which is highly sensitive. Confidentiality is something we can't mess with, or our reputation could be at risk."

"I understand completely," Pam said, nodding. "And that's why we take a similar approach to your team regarding information. Just as you do with our customer data, we share insights on trends, but we would never divulge information about individual companies. What else is on your mind?"

Again, Anne hesitated. "A lot is going wrong at Exalted, and while I'm sure Marketing isn't to blame, how can I be certain that something in your analytics won't mistakenly point a finger at us? I've got the full backing of one of our board members, Tom Ashcroft, and he would tear you *and* David apart if analytical errors found fault with his strategies."

"His strategies?" Pam asked, as casually as she possibly could.

"Well," said Anne, "As you may know, after I became CMO, our executive development program paired me with Tom Ashcroft. He turned out to be the best mentor, sponsor, and evangelist I could imagine. It's no secret that he pushed hard to have all marketing resources consolidated underneath me—brand strategy, advertising, the works."

Pam nodded intently, all her attention focused on Anne.

"But most importantly," the CMO continued, "his industry connections give him the inside track on what's happening in the marketplace. That's how he knew to persuade the board to stay the course in positioning Exalted as the premium brand. Some analysts are saying we should join the crowd of lower-cost providers, but he knows better. That's why I'm concerned that your analytics may lead to a false conclusion."

Pam nodded again. "I hear you, Anne. If I were in your position I would feel the same way. Let me assure you that we're just trying to understand what's happening in the business. You have my word that if we find anything that might point to issues with Marketing, you'll be the first to know; and I'll give you an opportunity to course-correct. I'm not out to make you, Tom Ashcroft, or anyone else look bad."

Seeing that Anne wasn't persuaded, Pam added, "We assume that everyone is operating with integrity and working their hardest to advance Exalted's interests and success. We just ask that you assume the same about us. My team and I will be straight with you."

Still reluctant, but out of reasons to stall, Anne agreed to send Marcus and Chloe the requested data. Pam responded: "Anne, thank you for your confidence in us. I'll keep you updated. And in the meantime, I hear you play a mean game of squash. How about we play before work next week at the athletic club down the street?"

The two executives put a date in their calendars, shook hands, and parted ways to continue with the day.

ONE MONTH POST OFF-SITE: MARCH 11

"You may or may not like what I'm about to present," said Chloe, lowering the lights so the group could better see her slides. "It's going to be an interesting morning."

Marcus, Elke, Sameer, and Martha, seated around the HR conference room table, looked at each other with apprehension. They each knew about one or more pieces of the puzzle Chloe was about to reveal, but none of them had the full picture except for Pam, who was unusually serious. She clearly knew what was coming, and with Chloe's ominous greeting, the group was on edge.

"As you all know," Chloe began, "I've spent the past month collecting, cleaning, and analyzing data based on the KPIs we brainstormed together. Here's the list of factors we put together." She flipped the switch on the projector.

"And the list of data to collect," Chloe said, advancing to the next slide:

SALES REP ATTRITION
KEY FACTORS

EMPLOYEE PERFORMANCE
(Rep Attainment)

QUOTA
DEVELOPMENT
MANAGER
LEADS
PRICE
PRODUCT(S)

EMPLOYEE ENGAGEMENT
(Rep Satisfaction)

COMPENSATION
MANAGER
OVERALL ENGAGEMENT

EMPLOYEE BRAND
(Rep Attraction)

INTERNAL REFERRALS
APPLICATIONS/ JOB
EXTERNAL RANKINGS
SOCIAL MEDIA

DATA TO COLLECT ON SALES REP ATTRITION

	STRUCTURED	UNSTRUCTURED
INTERNAL	• Quota — diff between quota potential and territory assigned • Strategic training coverage ratio — % of training resources covering top revenue drivers • Marketing Qualified Leads (MQL) — # leads passed to reps • Comp (base + commissions) • Manager ratings — individual: 360 reviews • Manager ratings — aggregate: engagement survey scores • # referrals (absolute # used in conversion ratio; larger accounts mean fewer referrals needed) • # job applicants per post	• Qualitative engagement survey feedback
EXTERNAL	• Employer ranking, e.g., Glassdoor • Price — difference between our product's price and the median price of all competitive products • Sales of organic vs. acquired vs. external products	• Glassdoor, other social media comments

"Pam had to pull a fair number of strings to make sure I got all the data I needed, and Marcus ran a lot of interference for me as well," Chloe continued, "but in the end, I did get everything, and even ended up going beyond this list."

Marcus and Chloe exchanged conspiratorial grins. It hadn't been easy to get that data, but they'd kept a positive attitude.

"And I also had help from some of Sameer's analysts and from some of the guys in Sales Ops. Bobby wasn't happy at first that I was working directly with one of his teams, but since we're solving his problem, Pam was able to convince him. I'll begin with the key finding that set everything in motion," Chloe stated. "Bobby had complained that his top reps were leaving, so I wanted to confirm that. As you'll see here, he was right." Chloe presented her next slide, "Top Performers Leaving at Alarming Rates."

"The attrition rate among top producers—that's the sales term for sellers—is more than twice that of low producers, which is increasing the overall sales rep attrition numbers," she reported. "As I said when we first met, 'why' is the most important word in analytics, and this chart definitely made me very curious. So I started to dig deeper, and I identified eight main factors impacting attrition. Here's a framework I have used for other HR projects, and these issues fit into it very well. I'm calling it the 'sales rep attrition ecosystem.'"

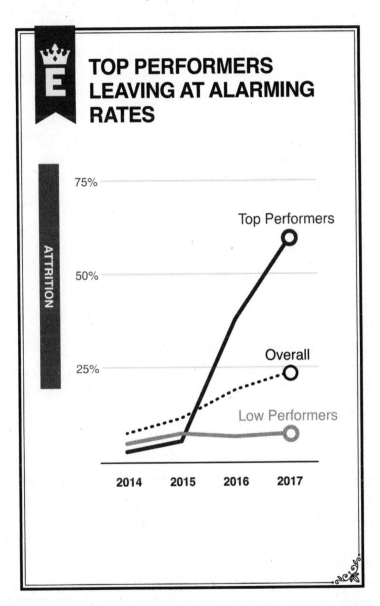

Chloe advanced to a slide depicting her ecosystem concept.

"Of these eight key factors," Chloe pressed on, "several have nothing to do with HR."

"What?!" cried Sameer. "Is this a rare opportunity for *schadenfreude*? The blame falling back into the laps of some of our worst critics?"

Pam, understanding Sameer completely and yet knowing the team was about to experience some blows, replied, "Let's not be too eager to gloat. We'll have plenty of our own opportunities for self-reflection. Walk us through it, Chloe."

"To summarize how I identified the top drivers of sales rep attrition," Chloe explained, "I analyzed more than 150 variables using univariate and multivariate analysis to understand the potential causes and the relationships between these variables and attrition. I included HR profiles, learning data, performance data, social media and external data, compensation, quotas, managers, and then I added to that mix exit interviews, engagement, retention, revenue, pricing, and other company data."

"I started with my models, which gave me correlations between KPIs, but not causal information. So I took the results and talked to experts on the ground so we could turn correlations into causations," Chloe continued. "Correlation versus causation is an important conversation, but let's hold off on that for now. What I've captured here are the statistically significant drivers. If we can take care of these, we just might make some serious headway toward fixing attrition."

COMPENSATION QUOTA
ATTAINMENT

PRODUCT   MANAGERS

**SALES REP
ATTRITION
ECOSYSTEM**

PRICE

ENABLEMENT

ENGAGEMENT

HIRING

The room fell silent as the team absorbed that HR could fix a huge company pain point, perhaps several. The stakes suddenly felt enormous. Pam was the first to smile, followed by Marcus, Sameer, Martha, and eventually Elke.

Chloe, sensing the momentum, continued. "The first key driver of sales rep attrition is compensation. As you might guess, as commission rates decrease, attrition rates increase. In other words, the further a rep is from making quota, the more likely he or she is to leave Exalted. But oddly, the reps with the lowest commission rates had the highest sales, as you can see in this slide."

"Asking why this was the case led me to an important discovery, which is the second key driver: quota. Look at these numbers," Chloe said, advancing to the next slide, which showed a clear yet surprising correlation between sales results and attrition.

"That doesn't make any sense," said Martha, shaking her head. "Why would reps who are bringing in ten times as much revenue as the lowest producers have a commission rate that's nearly 25 percent less?"

"I asked myself the same question," Chloe answered. "When you view it graphically, it's even more striking—and all the clearer that quotas for our best reps are set unrealistically high," she said, clicking ahead to a graph.

Pam added, "Chloe consulted with me about this because it's not intuitive what's happening here. It's not unusual to disproportionately increase quotas for the best reps, especially if the company is in a sales rut and analysts are expecting

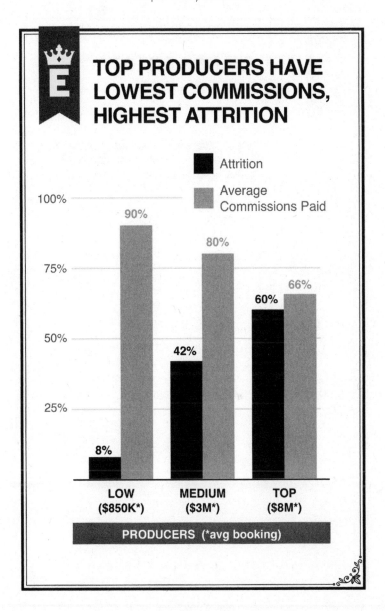

TOP PRODUCERS HAVE LOWEST COMMISSIONS, HIGHEST ATTRITION

- Attrition
- Average Commissions Paid

SALES REP ACTIVITY AND ATTRITION

	PRODUCERS		
	LOW	MEDIUM	TOP
AVERAGE BOOKING	**$850K**	**$3M**	**$8M**
AVERAGE QUOTA	$1M	$4M	$16M
AVERAGE ATTAINMENT	85%	75%	50%
AVERAGE COMMISSIONS PAID	90%	80%	66%
ATTRITION	8%	42%	60%

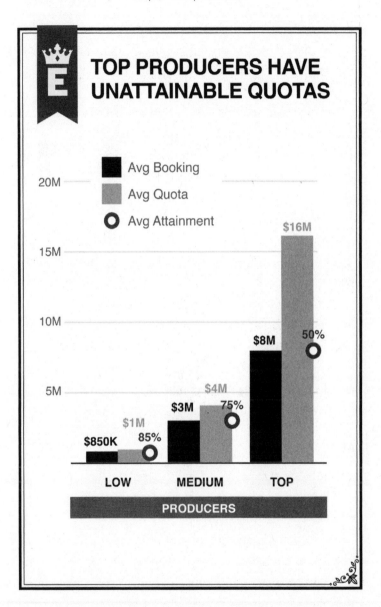

TOP PRODUCERS HAVE UNATTAINABLE QUOTAS

- Avg Booking
- Avg Quota
- Avg Attainment

20M

15M

10M

5M

$16M

$8M   50%

$4M

$3M   75%

$1M

$850K   85%

LOW   MEDIUM   TOP

PRODUCERS

a 30 percent revenue increase, but they somehow were set way too high. The low producers are likely new hires, who have smaller territories until they ramp up. That's standard practice."

"But how is it that no one ever noticed a discrepancy of $1 million versus $16 million in quota?" asked Martha, looking incredulous. "My comp team works with Sales Operations on base pay compensation levels, but they insist on setting quotas."

"We're not sure," answered Pam, "but Marcus and I are meeting with Bobby this afternoon to share these results and others with him so we'll know more after that. Chloe, what's next?"

"The third factor in the sales rep retention ecosystem," continued Chloe, "is the typical reason people leave a job: their manager. There are unfortunately too many sales managers who aren't very good at people management. Looking at exit interview data, I found that 90 percent of all people who have left rated their manager as the number one reason for leaving. Also, I found that people leave in clusters; the same managers consistently lose people, usually within twelve months of hire."

"What's going on there?" asked Martha, unsure she really wanted to know the answer.

"I looked at the attainment and promotion data for these managers, and discovered most were promoted within the past twelve to eighteen months, and all of them were high-performing sales reps—strong sellers who didn't necessarily have people management skills. And from the Learning Management System, I could see that none of them had completed any management training, probably because they were under pressure to be out in the field helping their teams to meet quota. I was able to look at aggregate engagement survey data on their direct reports, who consistently gave them low ratings on questions such as 'my manager contributes to my development.'"

"How many times have I told Bobby that people management skills are critical?" Martha groaned. "Maybe now he'll listen. But why weren't these managers flagged? Put on a performance improvement plan?"

"Given the pressure to increase sales," said Pam, "my guess is that these managers helped deliver revenue, so their lack of management skills was overlooked. We'll discuss it with Bobby."

"Martha," continued Chloe, "the somewhat good news is that experienced managers tend to have lower attrition numbers than untrained, newer managers. So that's further evidence that developing management skills makes a difference." Chloe advanced to the next slide.

"And further," said Chloe, advancing to the following slide, "I found that newer managers who were hired from the outside didn't have the same attrition issues as the internally promoted new managers. That's because they already had people management experience. So that goes toward confirming my theory that the difference was preparedness to coach and guide direct reports."

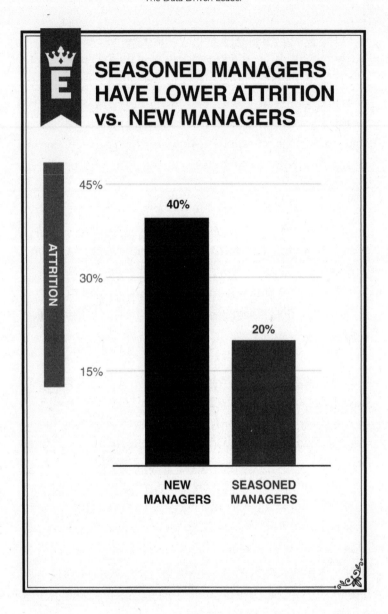

SEASONED MANAGERS HAVE LOWER ATTRITION vs. NEW MANAGERS

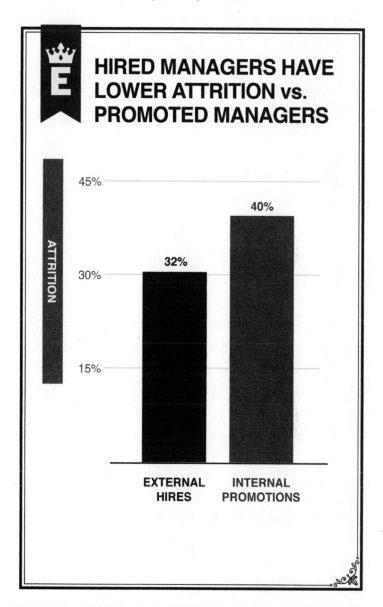

"I'm somehow feeling both vindicated and guilty," said Martha. "I feel like I failed these reps, which is terrible, but it's also really encouraging to know that training makes a difference. Maybe Bobby will start to see things differently."

"I think he will," said Chloe, advancing to the next slide. "The fourth key driver is enablement.

"Looking again at the DNA of our top sales reps, which I created using the techniques that Pam shared with me," Chloe continued, "I was able to identify the KPIs most closely associated with revenue impact. They appear here in order of their impact on sales. But there's a big disconnect."

"Look at these horizontal bars," Chloe continued, pointing at the screen. "They represent our enablement efforts for each KPI, based on the percentage of content in the LMS aligned to each KPI—all modalities of content, including instructor-led and self-paced. But the most content is on 'Sell Top Products,' and not on 'Lead Gen,' the most important KPI. If we can focus our enablement on these KPIs *in order of their importance* and track the outcomes, I believe we'd have measurable impact to show."

"I don't know about the rest of you, but I'm a believer," declared Martha. "I'm concerned that we haven't been training reps on the most important topics, but if data analytics can give me these kinds of insights, I'm all in. Marcus, tell me, will this sell Bobby on enablement? Sorry for the pun!"

"Ha ha. You are definitely not sorry about that pun, Martha, but yes, it's pretty compelling," answered Marcus. "I'm hopeful."

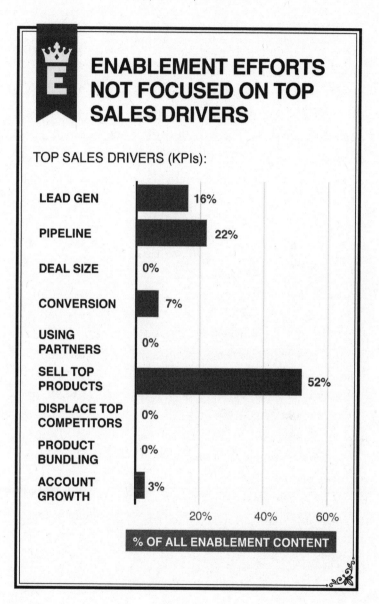

ENABLEMENT EFFORTS NOT FOCUSED ON TOP SALES DRIVERS

TOP SALES DRIVERS (KPIs):

LEAD GEN	16%
PIPELINE	22%
DEAL SIZE	0%
CONVERSION	7%
USING PARTNERS	0%
SELL TOP PRODUCTS	52%
DISPLACE TOP COMPETITORS	0%
PRODUCT BUNDLING	0%
ACCOUNT GROWTH	3%

20%   40%   60%

% OF ALL ENABLEMENT CONTENT

"Is it too early to be hopeful about hiring? I see that's next in the ecosystem," said Elke hopefully, looking up from the careful notes she'd been taking.

"We should be hopeful about all of it, Elke," responded Pam with a smile. "Let's think about these findings as opportunities to solve problems for the company and to improve our efficiency and effectiveness. But first let's take a short break. There's a lot more to cover."

SUMMARY

Chloe and Marcus encounter resistance as they begin to collect data to analyze. Pam must intervene with Chief Marketing Officer Anne Rodriguez, ultimately overcoming Anne's significant misgivings by asking, and answering, questions about her concerns. By doing so, she also learns that activist board member Thomas Ashcroft, Anne's mentor, has been pushing for Exalted to stay the course on its premium brand positioning.

A few weeks later, Chloe presents her findings to Pam's team, explaining and illustrating the descriptive and diagnostic analytics that helped identify the first four of eight key factors driving away the Exalted sales force in the "Sales Rep Attrition Ecosystem": compensation, quota, managers, and enablement. The team realizes that HR doesn't cause all HR-related issues, and that HR can help solve overall business problems.

COMMENTARY

IMPORTANT INITIAL STEPS

Any analytics journey will encounter times of amazing insights and times of absolute frustration. One example of the latter, which can stall many an analytics project before it ever gets off the ground, is someone blocking access to critical data.

A data owner may have legitimate reasons not to trust anyone else with access; sometimes, performing effective analytics requires data that is proprietary, valuable, confidential, and/or potentially damaging to an individual, group, company, or customer—or simply perceived as such. Data owners, being human, may be territorial, political, or just plain uncooperative.

The key, as Pam demonstrated with Anne, is to take time to explain to the gatekeeper why you are requesting the data and what you plan to do with it. Addressing Anne's concerns and gaining her buy-in was essential. One way to gain buy-in is to start out with an analytics project that will be enlightening to the organization without casting individuals or departments in a potentially negative light.

Here are some additional guidelines to keep in mind as you begin:

- **Start small and non-controversial.** This will allow you to gain some quick wins that identify process issues,[1] policies that could be improved or other triggers to company performance unlikely to prove contentious. Successfully identifying these early in your journey can go a long way toward building trust, enabling you to dive into much more sensitive topics down the road.

- **Understand the key players.** Know both them and their trusted relationships, particularly senior leaders, who may have strong ties with customers, board members, or investors. Taking the time to understand perspectives and alliances, as Pam did with Anne, can help to avoid catastrophic "door slamming" at a critical stage of a project.

- **Enlist key stakeholders early.** In our desire to solve problems swiftly, we may think we can—or should—do it on our own. Pam could easily have launched into solution mode with the authority given her by David, but any quick wins would likely be unsustainable. Even though Bobby is a reluctant partner at first, Pam's respectful persistence in gaining his understanding ends up a linchpin in her team's success, as we will find out later.

- **Slow down to speed up.** Human Resources people are trained to assess situations quickly and use their emotional intelligence to begin identifying "fixable" problems. In an effective data analytics project, however, invest in understanding the necessary inputs (just as our team identified the KPIs impacting attrition) or you run the risk of missing important insights that can help reveal the bigger picture.

- **Cast a wide net.** Look both inside and outside the company, and at structured (think Sameer's quantitative call center statistics) and unstructured data (think Sameer's recorded call center conversations). If you define your data sources too narrowly, your analysis will fail to produce meaningful insights and may even produce incomplete or erroneous results, which could lead to costly mistakes. For example, to understand why people are leaving your company, exit interview data alone likely won't suffice, as departing employees often give "safe" answers such as "leaving for more money" or "leaving for family reasons." They may not think anyone cares, not feel inclined to help, or, in an industry rife with mergers and acquisitions, not want to burn bridges. Data from third parties such as Glassdoor may provide more honest and actionable information, even if it can be painful.

- **Be patient.** Change takes time and requires the faith and cooperation of mere mortals. This is often truer for cutting-edge advancements like data analytics.

CONNECTING THE DOTS

As our characters start diving into the data in this chapter, they gain a greater understanding of the factors affecting their business and the dynamics behind the numbers. By asking the right questions and "slicing and dicing" the data, they begin to see the power of analytics and uncover correlations between KPIs they might not have noticed (or couldn't possibly have seen) before. It's essential to find and understand root causes rather than jumping to solutions that only treat symptoms.

At Exalted, Chloe identifies several counterintuitive outcomes that on the surface don't make sense, but she presses on. *Why* would the reps with the highest sales have the lowest commissions? Had she discarded that finding because it was counterintuitive, she would not have learned that their quotas were set unrealistically high, which also explained why these same reps had the highest attrition rate.

Similarly, Chloe uncovers that most sales reps left because of their manager, but had she stopped there—because that's *unsurprising*—she wouldn't have learned that the managers whose reps were most likely to quit were recently promoted and didn't complete manager training. Continuing to search and search and peel back the layers for the core "why" is at the heart of good quality analytics work.

Using the "ideal sales rep DNA" from Pam's project at Trajectory, Chloe can efficiently identify the key drivers of sales in order of impact. Many organizations, particularly established sales leaders, believe they know which KPIs lead to sales success. Perhaps CSO Bobby Cash felt it was selling top products, which might explain why more than half of all enablement content was on that topic. Yet only data analysis could yield an accurate list of the top revenue drivers, which will now allow Martha to reprioritize and rebalance training content.

Imagine how insights from a well-executed analytics exercise could allow you to enhance your effectiveness and input.

Go deeper on the four stages of analytics in Essential Reading, in the last section of this book. Feel free to flip ahead and read about diagnostic analytics, then return here and continue below.

CAUSATION VERSUS CORRELATION

When looking at relationships between KPIs, it's important to keep in mind that just because two variables are associated or correlated does not mean we can easily tell which one causes which. Sure, if we see that rain and wet grass always happen on the same day, it's easy to conclude that the rain caused the wet grass. But that's only because we have reliable experiential knowledge of weather's effects.

For more opaque processes, such as the functions of a large business, we should always question our first instincts. Does low employee engagement cause declining revenues? Or do declining revenues cause low engagement? Or is there some other hidden factor that causes both? We simply cannot tell from looking at a single figure.

Let's return for a moment to Chapter 2, when Pam's college basketball coach mentions that he has a talent scout assessment app that uses advanced analytics. This gives a nod to Michael Lewis' *Moneyball*,[2] which told the story of how the Oakland A's Billy Beane used sabermetrics[3] to build a winning baseball team on a shoestring budget.

A *Harvard Business Review* article[4] warns what happens when businesses ignore Lewis' *Moneyball* message about the twin dangers of relying on intuition and failing to understand the relationship between cause and effect.

- **Overconfidence bias.** People routinely overestimate their abilities, including their business judgment. Our confidence in intuitively knowing what is right is frequently at odds with reality.

- **Availability heuristic.** We tend to weight our judgments in favor of more recent information or on what we can readily recall (what is most available to us), thinking that can lead to flawed outcomes.
- **Status quo bias.** Doubling down on what we know, or preferring the status quo to the unknown, may lead us to manage with stale data or ignore indications of shifting metrics or performance drivers.

To avoid these perils, make sure that you collect a wide variety of KPIs, and then make judicious use of descriptive and diagnostic analytics.

NOTES

1. Josh Bersin, Karen O'Leonard, and Wendy Wang-Audia, *High-Impact Talent Analytics: Building a World-Class HR Measurement and Analytics Function* (Oakland, CA: Bersin & Associates, October 2013), 28, accessed May 25, 2017, http://www.bersin.com/Lib/Rs/ShowDocument.aspx?docid=16909.
2. Michael Lewis, *Moneyball: The Art of Winning an Unfair Game* (New York: W.W. Norton, 2003).
3. Any mathematical or statistical study of baseball (yes, that's a thing), according to the Society for American Baseball Research (also a thing). See Phil Birnbaum, "A Guide to Sabermetric Research," Society for American Baseball Research, accessed May 25, 2017, http://sabr.org/sabermetrics/single-page.
4. Michael J. Mauboussin, "The True Measures of Success," *Harvard Business Review*, October 2012, accessed May 25, 2017, https://hbr.org/2012/10/the-true-measures-of-success.

Chapter 5

DIAGNOSING WHAT'S WRONG

After the break, the group was chatty as they settled around the conference room table. The morning's revelations and what they might learn next about sales rep attrition energized the team. Pam nodded to Chloe to proceed.

"Welcome back, everyone. We've covered the first four factors in the sales rep attrition ecosystem: compensation, quota, manager, and enablement," said Chloe. "The fifth is hiring. To recap, it's been hard to replace good reps, it takes a long time to fill positions, and many new reps aren't successful and leave within the first year. Of course, the question is. . . ?" She paused expectantly.

"Why!" the group exclaimed, breaking into laughter.

"Yes!" Chloe exclaimed. "And sometimes, quantitative data isn't enough. You need the insights only humans can provide. This pushed me to survey current reps and managers and ask them what's going on. That gave me a lot of important clues. I also had conversations with Elke and some hiring managers."

Chloe continued: "I believe we've had issues getting and keeping competent reps for three reasons. First, the high attrition has kept Talent Acquisition too busy putting out fires to build a candidate pipeline, so filling nearly every vacancy means going out and looking for reps. Second, managers tend to tell TA about a vacancy only when they get notice from the employee, and that lack of lead time stretches out the search process."

"But . . . the third reason is where we start to see our opportunity," she said, looking apologetically at Elke. "We seem to have a big issue with candidate screening," she reported, advancing to the next slide as Elke braced for the worst.

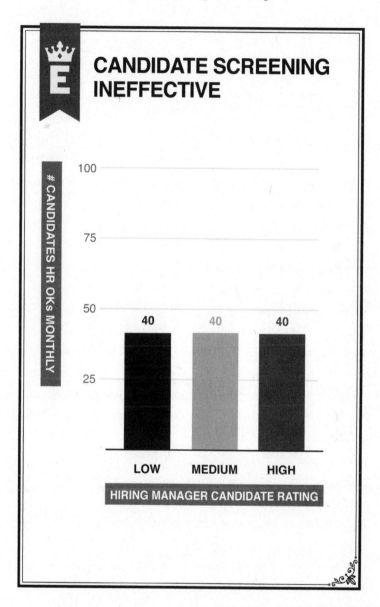

"This graph," Chloe explained, "shows that hiring managers are just as likely to rate the quality of candidates as low, medium, or high, meaning recruiters aren't focused on screening for high-quality candidates. And that's having a pretty significant impact on time to hire. Look," she said, continuing to the next slide, "# Days to Offer."

"Higher-quality candidates receive an offer in less than three weeks, but low-quality candidates might not be hired for nearly three months. Screening is slowing down hiring," Chloe concluded.

"Why wouldn't hiring managers just reject low-rated candidates?" asked Sameer.

"Yes, why indeed," Chloe declared. "A few hiring managers said that because there's pressure to fill spots, they don't reject candidates they rate as low; they mark them as 'refer' in the system, thinking maybe another manager might like them better. TA passes them on to another hiring manager, who does the same thing, until finally a hiring manager in a crunch offers the candidate a job. As you can imagine, these reps don't tend to succeed."

Elke sighed. "My department has always taken pride in setting a high target for our candidates-to-posting ratio," she said, "but it seems that's a disincentive to scrupulous screening. I'll start working on fixing that as soon as this meeting is over."

"Elke, that's great. But meanwhile we've got another problem with hiring that's out of your hands," said Chloe with a frown, advancing to the next slide.

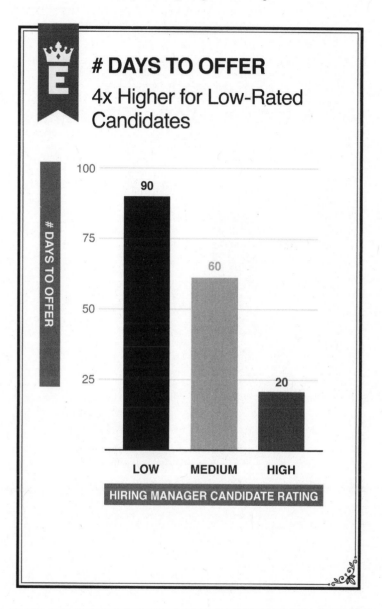

DAYS TO OFFER
4x Higher for Low-Rated Candidates

DAYS TO OFFER

LOW	90
MEDIUM	60
HIGH	20

HIRING MANAGER CANDIDATE RATING

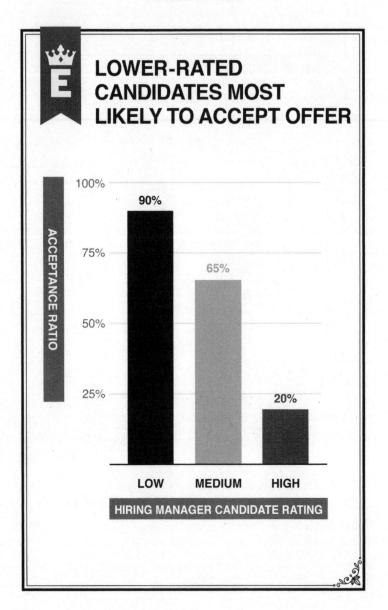

"This is one of the more troubling findings Chloe shared with me," Pam said, standing up. "High-quality candidates not accepting job offers typically means an issue with the employer brand. We can attribute some of that to our marketplace performance, but recent comments about Exalted on social media sources like Glassdoor are pretty awful. In addition to negative reviews around our interview process, which mirror a lot of what Chloe reported on today, some comments reflect the same sentiments as our engagement survey—that we have lost our way, that our leadership isn't tuned into reality, that there's not enough development or career opportunity—but the language used is much more . . . candid, shall we say?"

Sameer interjected, "But senior leadership doesn't care about engagement results. The company has always done so well that they felt they could ignore how employees are feeling."

"Maybe they're finally paying attention because things have gotten so bad," said Martha. "That's a shame. Last year at a senior leadership meeting, the previous CHRO and I shared a plan to improve engagement. The leaders seemed enthusiastic, but once sales started to dip they lost interest."

"That's not the first time an engagement plan was scrapped, either," added Marcus. "This company is great at many things, but paying attention to people metrics and issues has never been our strong suit."

"That's a great transition to our sixth factor, engagement," Chloe pronounced. "Let's look now at retention, the inverse of attrition. It's an accepted truth that engagement and retention decline in parallel, but at Exalted, this effect is amplified," she said, advancing to the next slide. "This chart shows that a 1 percent dip in engagement accompanies a 5 percent dip in retention. Engagement is a hugely important early predictor of retention."

"Maybe this will make our leadership pay closer attention," Sameer said with a scowl, crossing his arms.

"Well, unfortunately, I have something that they'll pay even closer attention to," Chloe said, advancing to the next slide.

Pam watched her team members' jaws drop. "Chloe," she said, "our C-suite will definitely be interested and will want to know how these parallel drops in engagement, retention and revenue are linked. That brings us to the service-profit chain. Please go to the next slide."

"The service-profit chain appeared in a 1994 *Harvard Business Review* article,"[1] explained Pam, "and although it was written about service organizations, a lot applies to Exalted. The authors argued that profit and growth come from customer loyalty, which results from customer satisfaction, which is influenced by services provided by employees, whose productivity, retention, and satisfaction depend on internal support services and policies. The bottom line: if we don't serve our employees well, the company won't grow."

"Pam, I've seen this model before and I'm personally a believer," said Marcus, "just as I believe in studies that show direct links between engagement and revenue. But proving it to our executives is another matter."

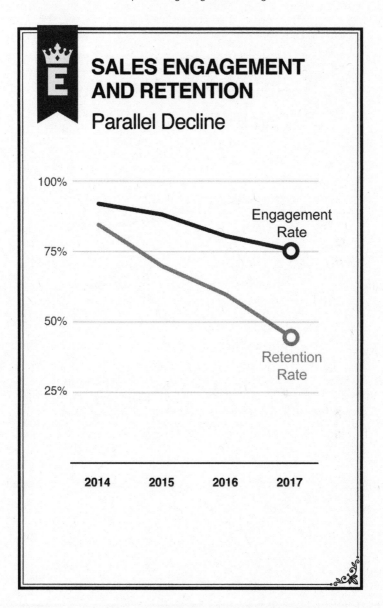

SALES ENGAGEMENT
AND RETENTION
Parallel Decline

Engagement
Rate

Retention
Rate

100%

75%

50%

25%

2014   2015   2016   2017

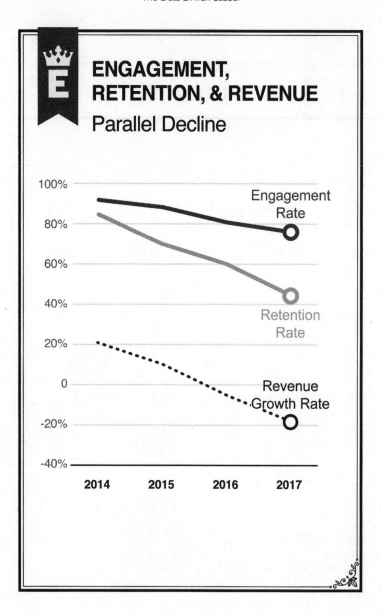

ENGAGEMENT, RETENTION, & REVENUE

Parallel Decline

SERVICE-PROFIT CHAIN

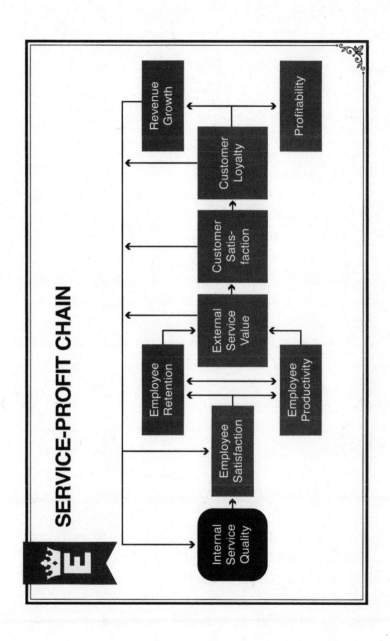

"I hear you, Marcus. Certainly, factors other than engagement impact revenue, as we'll hear from Chloe," answered Pam, "but I'm fairly sure Exalted leadership isn't aware of how dramatically retention, engagement, and revenue are plummeting in parallel. Combined with the service-profit chain and the studies you mentioned, it will be hard to refute that these issues are related."

"OK, Chloe, I'll bite," Martha volunteered. "*Why* is engagement taking such a nose dive?"

"Well, not surprisingly," Chloe answered, "for sales reps it's a combination of the factors we've been talking about. The lowest five employee engagement survey scores among disengaged reps are related to compensation, fair treatment, manager support, development opportunities, and belief in the company. But scores that trend downward so steeply generally indicate that either the company isn't doing anything in response to employee feedback—or what they are doing isn't working."

"Also," added Pam, "in the last few Exalted annual reports, the engagement numbers presented a pretty rosy picture. I assume that's because of pressure from above to gloss over the facts, something that can't continue. We need transparency and accountability about our survey results and how we're trying to improve them, or our scores will continue to suffer, as will our employer brand."

Marcus and Martha looked at each other in relief. They knew the previous CHRO had been ineffective, to say the least, at persuading Exalted leadership to deal with the company's engagement issues, and they even suspected the board was in the dark.

"You'll be pleased," announced Chloe, "that the last two findings have nothing to do with HR. The seventh ecosystem factor is price."

"I was right!" exclaimed Marcus in amazement.

"Yep," said Pam with a smile. "I told you all of you have great sales instincts. And Chloe has made yet another critical discovery with her analytics. Talk us through it."

"I got the first clues about pricing when I looked at exit interviews, engagement survey comments, and results from the manager/rep surveys I sent out," Chloe began. "A lot of reps said they couldn't sell our products because competitors are undercutting us. From this publicly available data, we are clearly still in the premium pricing tier relative to our next two biggest competitors," she said, advancing to the next slide.

"Notice that when Zenith Co. entered the market with a lower-priced product in 2015," Chloe continued, "Apex Inc. quickly responded by lowering its prices, and kept lowering them until they were actually below Zenith Co. But Exalted has basically stayed the course."

"I don't see the issue," Marcus admitted, looking perplexed.

"Well, charging premium prices only works if customers are willing to pay the premium, because the company is truly offering premium products—innovative and results focused. But that's not what's happening, based on this simple win/loss analysis using customer relationship management, or CRM, data," said Chloe, advancing to the next slide.

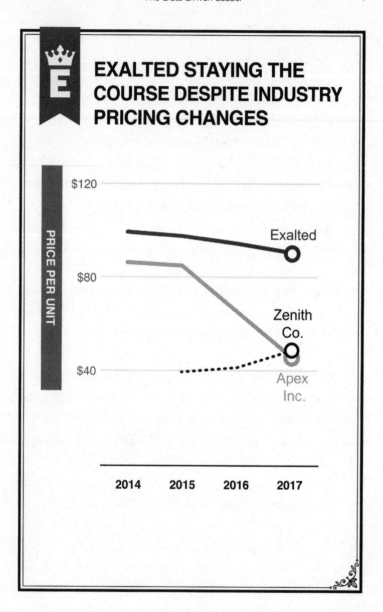

EXALTED STAYING THE COURSE DESPITE INDUSTRY PRICING CHANGES

PRICE PER UNIT

$120

$80

$40

Exalted

Zenith Co.

Apex Inc.

2014   2015   2016   2017

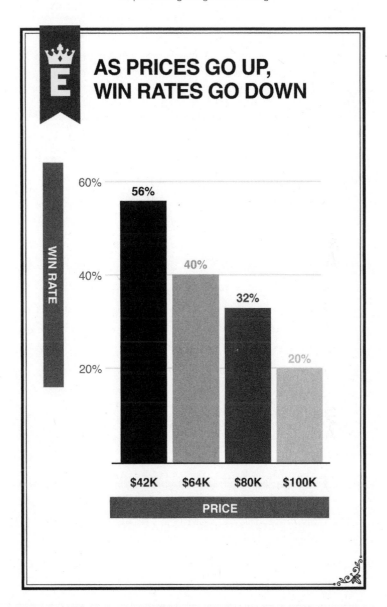

**AS PRICES GO UP,
WIN RATES GO DOWN**

WIN RATE

60%

56%

40%   40%

32%

20%   20%

$42K $64K $80K $100K

PRICE

"This supports the reps' claims," added Pam. "Chloe also looked at the 'loss reason' field in the CRM. She found that three years ago, price was the reason for losing 20 percent of deals. This year, it's up to 70 percent. I know sales leadership often dismiss reps who say prices are too high, so I also had Chloe look into industry reports comparing vendors, pricing rates, and products as well as the price/value ratio for each. Exalted is doing very poorly in these reports."

"But hasn't there been a lot of debate among analysts about Zenith Co. and whether their pricing model is sustainable?" asked Marcus. "It's true that some customers are moving toward lower-priced options, but that's just not what Exalted stands for."

"It hasn't been," Pam responded, "but that's changing. That's why Exalted has been on something of an acquisition spree in the past two years. The market is shifting toward new, fuller-functionality products that cost less and are easier to implement."

"But that's not what *our* customers want," Marcus insisted. "Bobby and I talk about this all the time. His leadership team thinks these competitors are going to fade quickly once the market realizes these new products are just part of a fad."

"Well," declared Chloe, "that brings me to the eighth and final factor impacting rep attrition: product. Marcus, yes, some analysts think Zenith Co. won't last, but others ding Exalted for being a dinosaur. And according to our CRM data, Exalted's acquired products, which are more similar in characteristics *and* price to those of Zenith Co. and other newer players, are significantly outselling our organically developed products."

"Given that we acquired those products *because* we weren't growing organically," added Pam, "that's a sign of success. But it also indicates that the market's interest in our legacy products is declining."

"But if we are offering competitively priced equivalents, why are our revenues continuing to sink?" asked Marcus, still trying to grasp the situation.

"Unfortunately, our challenge is more common than you might think," answered Pam. "And it's only easy for me to see because I've been in similar situations before, and because the data analysis that Chloe has done makes it fairly obvious. It boils down to change management, or more accurately, a lack of it. As I understand it, Exalted leadership made some well-considered shifts in strategy but then did a lousy job on implementation. They didn't really communicate the changes, gain buy-in, or update systems to support the new direction."

Martha interjected, "But my team developed sales training on the acquired products. I distinctly remember launching a series of product information sheets. They were exactly what Bobby asked for!"

"Martha, Exalted made a radical change in strategy," said Pam gently. "We have sales reps who've been selling our legacy product for decades. They can't just turn on a dime and sell acquired products that seem at odds with—as you put it, Marcus—what Exalted stands for. You also confirmed what I suspected, that Bobby and his team don't believe in the new direction, which is why they asked for product info sheets and not comprehensive training that would have changed mindsets, not just product bundles."

"And I never had any direction to change the kind of salespeople we were supposed to be hiring," exclaimed Elke, suddenly sitting upright. "No wonder so many of the new reps failed. We were hiring people to sell our legacy products."

"Is it possible that Bobby's team never changed the commission structure to incent reps to sell the acquired products?" asked Martha, her eyebrows drawing together in concern.

"You got it," said Pam. "Exalted leadership will need to get to the bottom of all of this, but for now I'll share two quotes with you. Chloe, next slide please."

Pam read the two quotes aloud, then added, "In other words, a successful strategy is only partly about the strategy. *Execution* determines the ultimate outcomes."

The team sat quietly, trying to absorb the information.

"But how . . . how is it possible that no one knew this until now?" asked Sameer, incredulous.

"There are so many possible reasons why a company's leadership doesn't see reality clearly," Pam replied. "Missing information, misinformation, misinterpreted information, selective filtering, self-preservation, bias, arrogance, denial, fear. . . . What has happened at Exalted could be any combination of those. Just take the example of how our engagement scores weren't accurately reported. Things like that happen in business all the time, and sometimes they balloon to the size of the issues we're facing now."

"Building a visionary company requires 1% vision and 99% alignment."

– Jim Collins and Jerry Porras,
Built to Last

"Culture eats strategy for breakfast."

– attributed to Peter Drucker

"So . . . what should we do?" Marcus asked, stunned. He, Martha, Elke, and Sameer all turned to look at Pam. She smiled confidently.

"Guys, I'm very optimistic," Pam stated matter-of-factly. "The first step toward solving any problem is understanding that problem, and although our leadership won't have an easy time accepting everything we've discussed today, we've done a tremendous service for Exalted shareholders and, more importantly, its employees. Also, this team only needs to fix what's in our domain, and we have Chloe to help us pinpoint how to focus our efforts."

Taking Pam's cue, Chloe nodded and gave a warm and buoyant smile at each member of the group. She also knew the road ahead wouldn't be easy, but she had complete faith in Pam's leadership.

"Chloe has already started on the next phase of our analytics work, which is determining where we should begin our own efforts to turn things around," Pam shared. "I'll need you to clear your schedules for a two-day off-site next week to flesh out our plan and next steps. Meanwhile, I have meetings lined up with Bobby and Anne Rodriguez today, followed by the others tomorrow."

As the team packed up, looking drained, Elke turned to Marcus and whispered, "Why do I suddenly feel nauseated?"

"Maybe because we just got off a big surprise roller-coaster ride," Marcus thought to himself, already bracing himself for the wrath of Bobby Cash.

LATER THAT DAY . . .

Pam and Marcus sat quietly across from Bobby as he went red-faced, fists clenched, leaning forward on his desk, trying to gather his thoughts. They had just shared with him Chloe's deck on the sales rep attrition ecosystem, breaking the news as gently as they could, and he was uncharacteristically at a loss for words.

Finally, Bobby spoke, his anger controlled but very present. "Has my team seen this? Was anyone involved in putting this so-called ecosystem together? How can I know this is for real? I mean, how can this possibly be for real?!"

"Your team helped us compile these numbers," Pam calmly answered. "You provided us with support from your head of sales ops and some of his analysts gave Chloe a hand in pulling the data and running some reports. But they haven't seen these results yet. We're bringing them to you first. And we want to partner with you to figure out what to do next."

"Hey, I've been earning big money for me and all the companies where I've worked for my entire career," Bobby said, regaining his composure. "If I've got some loser reps who can't sell, that's not my fault. I have to keep my territories covered and TA keeps sending me C players. Not even B players! There's too much half-assed work being done around here. Our product group can't seem to design anything half-decent. It's embarrassing to have to keep explaining to customers why we have to acquire companies to put out new products."

"Bobby, this was pretty surprising to me, too," Marcus confessed, "but there's plenty of blame to go around, and unfortunately you and I will need to give some hard thought to how we can address where we might have gone wrong."

Bobby's eyes widened and his lips tightened.

"Marcus is right, Bobby," Pam added. "Making decisions without the right data has happened all over Exalted. You're in good company with most of our leadership. And with most leaders in most companies, according to all the reports I've read about how infrequently data analytics is used."

"Yeah, well I've never needed any damned data before," Bobby scowled. "And we've always managed just fine without wasting time on training. You can't teach sales. Either you were born to do it or you weren't."

"I agree with you that there's some innate talent required," said Pam, "but I've seen plenty of evidence that training can work when analytics are used to pinpoint what reps need to learn to be successful. We can do that here, now. Bobby, we've got no training on four out of the top nine factors impacting rep revenue—it's only logical that we change that."

Bobby crossed his arms, frowning. "I suppose you've talked to David and are ready to take over when I get booted out. You couldn't really have come here to head up HR, Pam," he scoffed.

"I haven't talked to David. I don't want to talk to him without you, and I'm not after your job," Pam countered. "I don't want to try to solve this without you, and I won't abandon you to fix this on your own. It will only work if we approach it side by side. I'd love to talk through some ideas with you and hear your input, and then we can present them to David together."

She thought she could see Bobby's defenses start to lower, but she wanted to be sure.

"Of course, I don't want to waste your time if you're not interested in partnering."

After a pause, Bobby started to soften. "Look, this is a lot to take in at once. Give me some time to digest it and get comfortable with it. It's a really different way to look at the business. Cut me some slack."

"I know it's fast," Pam replied, "but I need to know that I have your buy-in. I don't want to find out two months from now at a leadership meeting that you and I weren't aligned."

Bobby sighed. "Jeez, Pam, give me a little breathing room. I'm with you, but don't rush me too much."

"I appreciate your openness," Pam said with a nod and a warm smile. "Now I have to go break the news to Anne."

"That's gonna be tough," Bobby replied. "You likely heard from David that Anne is pretty tight with that board member Ashcroft. To change her mind, you'll have to change his mind. And if you ask me, that guy is taking his activist investor role a little too seriously. Maybe I should come with you? I know Anne and how to talk to her."

"Bobby, it's very generous of you to offer," Pam said, hiding her surprise at his apparent about-face. "Let us talk to her alone first. I don't want her to feel like we're ganging up on her. She and I have developed a good rapport, but it will still be a hard pill to swallow. Let's talk again later this week?"

"That's a plan, Pam. Let me know how it goes with Anne. And Marcus, we may need a little extra time for our weekly meeting."

A SHORT TIME LATER ...

Both Pam and Marcus experienced a keen sense of déjà vu as they watched Anne's response to the ecosystem deck. Anne's lips were pursed and her expression grim as she scrutinized the printed slides on pricing Pam had supplied as a leave-behind. After a few long moments, she removed her reading glasses and clasped her hands together on the small meeting table in her office.

"Do you *know* that we're in the top right quadrant of all the market dynamics reports, and that we're at the *highest* end of the price curve because that's our brand strategy?" asked Anne forcefully, not waiting for a reply. "If Bobby's team knew how to sell value, we wouldn't be in this situation. We don't sell on price, we sell on our premium offering," she snapped.

"Anne, neither of us are pricing experts. We just know what the data says," Pam replied gently.

"We'll never win at the low end of the market," Anne declared, her voice beginning to rise. "We tried selling a commodity product a few years ago, and it failed completely. Our customers expect high quality. As Tom Ashcroft loves to say, 'We are the Maserati of this market.' And market research says customers are more than willing to pay for that."

"Market research can be wrong. I've seen it before," Pam countered, remaining steadfast but friendly. "But the data gives us a clear picture of reality as it actually is: most our customers and prospects look for value and features. The information in your hands confirms what we heard from both low- and high-performing sales reps."

"Well, Tom is convinced that we should stay the course," Anne said, digging in her heels. "He can be abrasive but he knows this field and clearly has a stake in the company succeeding. He wouldn't steer us off course."

"Anne, I understand where you're coming from and I completely agree that Tom has Exalted's best interests at heart," Pam replied. "I've also learned that data often contradicts opinions, even from experts. That doesn't mean the data is incorrect. But why don't you take a closer look at the charts and let me know what you think? You might see something we missed that could be very valuable."

Anne was running out of reasons to protest when Marcus jumped into the conversation. "We're here to work together to figure this out, Anne. We'll partner with you like we just agreed to partner with Sales."

"Bobby?! You showed him these numbers? What did he say? Did he throw my team under the bus?" she demanded.

"Like you, he was surprised and not very happy, but he's open to using data to find root causes and how to address them," Marcus answered. "We're about to have a similar conversation with the Product team leaders and hope they'll want to join you and Bobby in figuring out how to use this information wisely, not blame each other."

"He didn't cast blame? That's not the Bobby I know," said Anne, taken aback.

"Data takes emotions out of the conversation," Pam stated. "He's not a complete believer yet, but we're getting there. Let's be tough on the issues, using data and facts to objectively see what those issues are, and then we won't feel any need to be tough on each other."

Anne lowered her head for a moment and then looked up. "Guys, I'm under so much pressure. I've got David and the board breathing down my neck, and Tom gives me pep talks nearly every week about not straying from the company legacy. People are going to freak out. How could I possibly position this as anything else than retreating from our market position? I've been telling people for years to sell value and not to discount. Put yourself in my shoes."

"Anne, we hear you," Pam replied, "but we aren't the first company to overlook changing realities, and we won't be the last. What matters is course-correcting, together, before it's too late."

Anne sat back for a long pause, thinking. "OK, if Bobby is willing to give you a hearing, I am, too. But Tom Ashcroft is another matter. It's never easy to get him to consider another approach. But let me talk to him. I know him best."

Pam and Marcus thanked Anne and agreed to meet with David together to present the findings after Anne had time to review them and they'd come up with a few potential strategies to propose. After shaking hands and heading out of her office, Marcus turned to Pam.

"Are you sure you can handle Ashcroft? I've never met him, but he has quite a reputation."

"You can't argue with facts, Marcus," said Pam, radiating confidence.

"Yep, but he'll undoubtedly try," Marcus thought to himself.

JUST AFTER 5:30 P.M. . . .

Pam had just waved goodbye to her assistant when her office line rang. She picked up the phone, and immediately the voice on the other end of the line began to bellow: "And just who do you think you are?!"

"Mr. Ashcroft," answered Pam pleasantly. "I've been expecting your call. How are you this afternoon?"

"Don't mess with me, Sharp," answered Thomas Ashcroft curtly. "You can try messing with Anne and Bobby, but you're out of your league with me. You were brought in to fix HR, not to meddle in other departments, so you'd better stay in your own swim lane. I have been working with Anne for more than a year now, and she's on track."

"Sir, with all due respect, Exalted is far from on track," Pam said quietly but firmly.

"You know, I've heard good things about you from David," Ashcroft continued with a sneer, "but you've been here for less than a full quarter and you're already making a lot of accusations about what's wrong. David knows the board is keeping a very close eye on everything that's happening, and I'm one of the more influential people on the board. So be careful about throwing data around without knowing what the hell you're talking about."

And with that, he slammed down the phone.

Pam loved a good challenge, and hers had just become more interesting. Now, she thought, I know what David meant when he said the situation was serious. Time to put this project into high gear and bring the facts to light.

SUMMARY

Chloe continues to present her findings to Pam's team, and how she used descriptive and diagnostic analytics to identify the last four key factors behind the "sales rep attrition ecosystem": hiring, engagement, pricing, and product. A clearer picture of what's been driving away reps begins to emerge. While some root causes are HR-related flaws, what's truly dragging down Exalted is a classic senior leadership mistake. The company began to shift direction, but failed to enact careful change management throughout the organization. Pam and Marcus share the discoveries with Bobby and Anne, who both initially respond with shock and denial but are persuaded by the data and Pam's partnership approach. Anne insists that she communicate the news to her mentor and board member Thomas Ashcroft. That conversation prompts an angry phone call from Ashcroft to Pam; our heroine is unsurprised, unshaken, and determined to set Exalted back on the right course.

COMMENTARY

GETTING TO THE WHY (AND WHAT COMES AFTER)

In this chapter, Pam and Chloe dive deeper into the specifics of sales rep attrition. These specifics help to further reveal how analytics can uncover the "why" behind issues in an organization.

In the hiring realm, for example, Chloe points out the importance of qualitative data. To better understand the descriptive reporting (detailed in the previous chapter), she surveys reps and managers about the current situation. That reveals why it can take so long to replace reps who quit: a combination of an empty talent pipeline, misguidance from efficiency KPIs, hiring managers untrained in hiring, and, ultimately, pressure to just fill the role. The numbers alone didn't explain the "why" on any of these. You are likely to face similar scenarios and will need to complement numerical data with human-supplied facts and insights.

It's critical that Pam, Elke, and the team fix hiring. Organizations must not bring in suboptimal new employees just to fill requisitions. This is perhaps the most damaging decision a company can make, as it lowers the bar for performance and damages long-term viability, cripples the culture, and eats time and cash.

Chloe and team also discover another classic senior leadership mistake: ignoring employee engagement numbers, especially ones that are clearly trending downward. In organizations like Exalted that are struggling, leaders cannot take shortcuts and ignore valuable data and insights. Martha points out that, although senior leadership paid lip service to the idea of an engagement plan, they put it on the back burner as soon as a "more important" issue arose.

Simply reporting that employees are not engaged, however, is unpersuasive. HR leaders wanting to get the full attention of executives must speak the language the C-suite understands: business. *Present the business case.* Explain in dollars and cents the impact of low engagement on productivity, profitability, and customer satisfaction. Chloe does this with a graph showing retention, engagement, and revenue all plummeting. Simultaneously, Pam illustrates with the Service-Profit Chain that an organization must serve its employees well to grow. (See "Engagement, Retention, and Revenue," below, for the studies Marcus mentioned and data linking engagement and business outcomes.)

Importantly, as our story shows, engagement is *not* the exclusive domain of Human Resources. Many factors can impact engagement, including ones seemingly unrelated, such as market dynamics. The biggest revelation of Chloe's research turns out to be Exalted leaders' near-fatal misstep: enacting a deeply transformative strategy shift to lower-cost, acquired products without meticulous change management! Many in leadership roles, including the CSO and a key board member, didn't even support the new strategy. Yet this happens more often than you might imagine. The technology industry, for example, is littered with once-great companies that missed key market turns due to inadequate focus on change management, lack of awareness, arrogance, miscommunication, fear, and any number of other human foibles.

At Exalted, rep complaints about high prices were heard as excuses by those who believed in the premium provider approach. Bobby Cash and his team were so convinced that they only asked Martha's Learning & Development group to produce product sheets for Exalted's acquired products— a sure sign that they weren't serious about selling them. But, of course, the market had evolved and the competition began to rapidly take Exalted's market share.

In today's ultra-competitive market, the best organizations are obsessed with what's next. Those that not only survive but thrive think a minimum of eighteen to twenty-four months out. This requires close connections with customers, who drive market trends. If, as with Exalted, the best sales reps with the strongest relationships with top customers were leaving, that conduit of information was rapidly disappearing. The reps who stayed kept selling only what they knew, not the newest and most innovative products. This failure compounded the issues around market share, profitability, and customer retention.

Many senior leaders, like Anne, believe they have accurate data. They steadfastly hold onto what they see as irrefutable market truths without realizing that the data may represent only a point in time or where the market was, not where it is going or what it means within the broader context of other data sets.

These are often very emotional conversations that can shake people's confidence and long-held beliefs. Pam does an excellent job of conveying to Bobby and Anne that this is a partnership, not a crusade, and although Tom Ashcroft doesn't give Pam a chance to reply, she'll eventually have to win him over as well. Ultimately, she'll let the data speak for itself. It is much harder to refute data than intuition.

PRACTICAL CHANGE MANAGEMENT

Too many companies devote significant attention to the technicalities of data analytics while overlooking a core truth of the human condition: resistance to change. Because it challenges the old ways of doing things, and until someone has experienced its power and benefits, data analytics can provoke a host of negative responses: fear, intimidation, skepticism.

As an analytics project progresses and the successes accumulate, however, many skeptics become believers. Some will even become ambassadors and champions. Thus, implementing transformational change requires strong, thoughtful leadership. When planning a data analytics initiative, you may want to keep these principles in mind:

- Gain buy-in from the beginning by talking to everyone involved and inviting their participation.
- Tell them, tell them again, and then tell them again. People need to read and hear information several times to become comfortable with new ideas, with time and space in between to process the change.
- Understand the Kübler-Ross Change Curve (sometimes called the change acceptance curve)—where you came

from, where you are, and what's coming up next in your change journey.[2]

- Include detractors in the inner circle of your team. Consider making your biggest detractor your chief lieutenant. If relevant, hold him or her accountable for successfully carrying out assigned change-related responsibilities.
- Search for people who can be helpful. Be a connector. Conduct skip-level meetings all over the organization. Don't simply recruit people according to title or position. Look for the influencers and people who are doing amazing, cool, impactful work.

ENGAGEMENT, RETENTION, AND REVENUE

On Chloe's chart, engagement, retention, and revenue are all steeply declining. It may be tough for her to prove causation without external research; fortunately, there are plenty of such findings. Here are a few, in case your executives are not aware, or convinced, of the links. For example, the Hay Group reports that organizations in which employees are highly engaged experience 40 percent less employee turnover.[3]

Gallup found that highly engaged business units:

- Realize a 41 percent reduction in absenteeism
- Are 17 percent more productive
- Lose fewer employees, with 59 percent less turnover in organizations with less than 40 percent annualized turnover
- Achieve a 20 percent increase in sales
- Generate 21 percent greater profitability[4]

According to research from Aon Hewitt, consistent, statistically significant relationships exist between higher levels of employee engagement and financial performance.

- There is a positive correlation between increased employment engagement and revenue growth in the following year: a 5 percent rise in engagement is linked to a 3 percent growth in revenue.
- When combined with strong leadership, reputations, and performance orientation, strong employee engagement drives incremental business performance in sales, operating margin, and total shareholder return beyond top-quartile employee engagement alone.[5]

Finally, CEB, Inc., reports that companies with employee engagement levels in the top 25 percent outperform those in the bottom 25 percent in return on assets (7 percent versus –5 percent) and profitability (7 percent versus –4 percent).[6]

NOTES

1. James L. Heskett, Thomas O. Jones, Gary W. Loveman, W. Earl Sasser, Jr., and Leonard A. Schlesinger, "Putting the Service-Profit Chain to Work," *Harvard Business Review*, 1994, republished July/August 2008, accessed May 10, 2017, https://hbr.org/2008/07/putting-the-service-profit-chain-to-work.
2. "The Change Curve," University of Exeter, accessed May 25, 2017, http://www.exeter.ac.uk/media/universityofexeter/humanresources/documents/learningdevelopment/the_change_curve.pdf.

3. As cited in Brenda Kowske, *The Employee Engagement Primer* (Oakland, CA: Bersin & Associates, January 2012), 7, accessed May 25, 2017, http://www.bersin.com/Lib/Rs/ShowDocument.aspx?docid=15197.

4. Jim Harter and Annamarie Mann, "The Right Culture: Not About Employee Happiness," *Gallup Business Journal*, last modified April 12, 2017, accessed May 25, 2017, http://www.gallup.com/businessjournal/208487/right-culture-not-employee-happiness.aspx?version=print.

5. Ken Oehler, *2015 Trends in Global Employee Engagement* (London: Aon plc, 2015), 1, accessed May 25, 2017, http://www.aon.com/attachments/human-capital-consulting/2015-Trends-in-Global-Employee-Engagement-Report.pdf.

6. "Rethinking the Workforce Survey" (Arlington, VA: CEB Global, 2015), 7, accessed May 25, 2017, https://www.cebglobal.com/content/ dam/cebglobal/us/EN/talent-management/workforce-surveys/pdfs/ws-fwe-rethinkingtheworkforcesurvey-clearadvantage-wp.pdf.

Chapter 6

THE ROAD AHEAD

MARCH 25 (TWO WEEKS LATER . . .)

The team was in high spirits as they convened in the conference room. Marcus and Chloe chatted about data collection as she plugged her enormous laptop into the projection console. Sameer and Pam made each other laugh as they made plans to pare down a very long list of monthly reports. Martha and Elke excitedly discussed the upcoming half-day off-site for their two teams to address enhancing their communication and collaboration.

Pam called the team to order. "Thank you all for your hard work over the last few weeks," she began. "I'm looking forward to the details of your plan. First, here's a recap of our ecosystem list and the status of projects outside our domain." She motioned to Chloe, who revealed the first slide.

"As you can see," she continued, "in response to the ecosystem, Sales is about to announce changes to quotas and is working with Marketing on new incentives for selling our acquired products. The product team has ramped up development of internal products in addition to continuing our acquisition strategy and figuring out how to integrate acquired products into Exalted's overall architecture. They may be under the greatest pressure of all. Chloe, David, and the leadership team agree that you have made a huge impact on this company with your analytics discoveries. Let's hear what's next."

"Thank you, Pam," Chloe replied with pride. "I'm lucky to have such great partners," she said, nodding to the team. "The Sales Operations people have also been very helpful. As you know, we had a two-day brainstorming, which yielded a solid action plan. We identified three HR data analytics initiatives we feel will yield the highest ROI and turn things around fastest." Chloe advanced to the next slide.

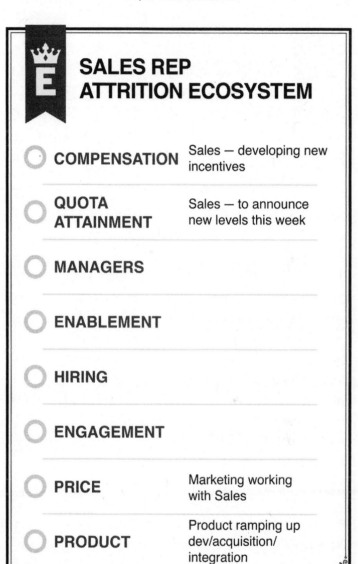

SALES REP ATTRITION ECOSYSTEM

COMPENSATION — Sales — developing new incentives

QUOTA ATTAINMENT — Sales — to announce new levels this week

MANAGERS

ENABLEMENT

HIRING

ENGAGEMENT

PRICE — Marketing working with Sales

PRODUCT — Product ramping up dev/acquisition/integration

SALES REP
ATTRITION ECOSYSTEM

○ COMPENSATION — Sales — developing new incentives

○ QUOTA ATTAINMENT — Sales — to announce new levels this week

○ **MANAGERS**

○ **ENABLEMENT**

○ **HIRING**

○ **ENGAGEMENT**

○ PRICE — Marketing working with Sales

○ PRODUCT — Product ramping up dev/acquisition/integration

"It's all interrelated," said Marcus enthusiastically. "So we are attacking all of this as a team and continuing to execute in partnership with Sales Ops."

"Did I hear you mention Sales?" boomed a voice from the doorway. "Then I guess I'd better come on in."

"Bobby, good of you to join us," said Pam, rising to shake his hand. "Glad you could make it. I figured you'd want to hear what we're all up to."

"The preview from my Sales Ops leader sounded pretty good," said Bobby. "I've still got my doubts, but since my people are happy, I couldn't resist your invitation to see for myself. Go on, Chloe. I've heard good things about you."

Pam introduced Chloe and Bobby, with surprised smiles from the rest of the team, and after a handshake Chloe continued.

"Our overall goal is ensuring Bobby has enough talented reps to get revenue up," she summarized, recapping the initial challenge. "That'll mean keeping and developing the best reps we have, and bringing in great new talent. Our first two initiatives are separate but related approaches to stem rep attrition."

"Realignment of quotas coming from Bobby's team should help," Chloe continued, as Bobby nodded. "But we still need to stop the bleeding. Analytics can help us find the top reps at risk of leaving; then we can persuade them to stay. We'll also identify low performers likely to leave and support them reaching quota. Under normal circumstances, we might exit them compassionately, but we can't afford to lose anyone else right now, and we need to take some pressure off of hiring managers and Talent Acquisition."

STEM REP ATTRITION
KEY ANALYTICS
INITIATIVES

RETAIN
focus on top and bottom reps

DEVELOP
with targeted enablement

HIRE
great new reps

Marcus chimed in, "We'll do what Chloe calls retention risk analysis—looking at the profiles of reps who've quit and find the reps with similar profiles. Then we'll help their managers work to keep them. It's talent retention supported by data. Of course, Chloe will have to explain the details."

"Nicely put, Marcus," Chloe responded. "We can also use analytics to help predict which managers need help, either because they fit the profile of managers whose team members tend to quit, or because they have a team at risk of missing quota. Then those managers will receive coaching and support from *their* managers."

"We'll start with mandatory manager intervention training, based on the key factors causing reps to stay or leave, which we know from exit interviews and Chloe's surveys," Martha interjected. "For example, we'll train managers on how to be more supportive and more effective at coaching their reps on key revenue-driving KPIs to help them hit quota. Longer term we'll add these and other topics to all leadership development programs, develop new criteria for hiring and promoting managers, and also get serious about succession planning. I'm also thrilled to share that Bobby has agreed to make new manager training mandatory."

"Chloe's numbers were persuasive," said Bobby. "I hate taking reps out of the field, but it will be worth it if we can get our managers to develop and lead winning teams. I'd also *love* to get off the hiring hamster wheel."

"Thanks for the segue to hiring, Bobby," Chloe said. "We also need to quickly replace the reps who have left. We can use analytics to identify quality candidates based on Exalted's ideal sales rep DNA, which gives us specific quantitative info to go on, versus just standard quality measures like GPA or where they worked."

"And check this out!" exclaimed Elke. "We can even identify the candidates most likely to accept our offer. Chloe will explain it, but I think it's pretty amazing. We can also use the ideal sales rep DNA to update our hiring criteria and from there tailor interview questions and develop a candidate scoring system. That should help us find quality candidates faster and onboard reps more likely to succeed. I, for one, am pretty excited."

"If what Elke is saying is true, I'm taking us all to see the Bulls play in the semi-finals," Bobby declared, obviously impressed. "I had no idea we could do all that."

"We *should* be able to do that with the direct involvement of you and your team, yes," Chloe responded. "Let's review our detailed plans for using analytics to address engagement, manager, and hiring issues. We're building on the sales rep attrition ecosystem, which mostly used descriptive analytics. Bobby, I can bring you up to speed separately on the four stages of analytics."

"Aw, don't you worry about me," said Bobby, "Pam's already given me some solid reading material so I'm nearly a guru in the four stages. Next is diagnostic, right?" he asked with a wink.

Pam was both taken aback and delighted at how quickly Bobby had changed his attitude, and with how effortlessly he was now charming her team. "Bobby, you've got tough competition in this room for fiercest analytics advocate, but I'd say you're in the running," she said with a wide smile. "Go on, Chloe."

"Bobby, you're absolutely right. Next, we'll be using diagnostic analytics, followed by predictive and prescriptive. The first example is our talent retention risk analysis," Chloe explained, advancing to the next slide.

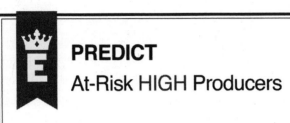

PREDICT
At-Risk HIGH Producers

Not meeting quota

Commission lower than previous year

Not actively creating pipeline

Not doing renewal deals

Not completing development plan

Reports to manager with high
team attrition

"We'll identify two types of at-risk reps, high producers and low producers," she continued. "Starting with high producers, you see here some of the factors associated with attrition—these are the leading indicators. We'll use diagnostic analytics to review the profiles of top reps who've quit and then identify which top reps might leave based on their similarities."

"OK, I'm all for analytics, but to be honest," said Bobby, "that list is pretty intuitive. Even obvious. Are you sure we need to run a bunch of numbers to figure that out? I'm asking sincerely. Educate me."

"That's a great question, Bobby," Chloe replied. "Sometimes factors are less obvious than we think, and without analysis it's hard to tell which factors have more of an impact. This slide lists only six factors, but we started with dozens, many of which also looked intuitive. Plus, analytics can provide early warning so we can take action before it's too late. Speed is also key. Figuring out which reps were at risk without analytics would take a long time."

"I see your point," said Bobby. "I suppose, being honest here, if it was so obvious, we could have prevented all those reps from leaving. So how do predictive analytics work exactly, so I can expand my already *tremendous* knowledge of this subject?"

"Sure thing, Bobby," responded Chloe. "Basically, we are predicting the future based on the past. Spam filters are a pretty common example of predictive analytics—they filter out emails that are similar to ones proven to be junk. Product recommendations on Amazon are similar. Using information

156

on you and other customers like you, their algorithms can predict what you might want to buy. It's like a farmer who plants five different kinds of seeds and sees how they grow. The next year, that farmer can plant the seeds that yielded better outcomes."

"What we'll do from a technical perspective," Chloe continued, "is build an analytics model and then feed it data, which is information on our reps, their profiles, and past performance. We then 'train' the model to compare the historic data to data on current reps and identify which reps are most similar. Let's go on to low producers. The same principles apply."

"Some of these factors may seem obvious, as well," Chloe continued, advancing to the next slide, "but manually identifying dozens of reps matching these criteria would be, well…."

"A nightmarish time suck," Bobby said wryly. "And ordinarily I wouldn't make *any* effort to hold onto low performers, but we can't afford to lose anyone else, and some of these reps do have a relationship with our customers, however minimal. I hope that as we get our house in order on comp and quota and, yes, Martha, start getting people into training, we'll separate the men from the—I mean, the wheat from the chaff. Then the folks who are really not gonna make it will say *sayonara*."

"I agree," said Pam. "Let's help our struggling reps, especially since we need them right now and, of course, because they deserve a fair chance. But if they're not successful, even with the right tools and support, then exiting them compassionately is the way to go."

157

PREDICT
At-Risk LOW Producers

Joined within past 12 months

Not on track to meet quota

Not successful creating pipeline

Not completing training courses

Reports to manager with high
team attrition

PREDICT
MANAGERS at Risk of Losing Reps

Promoted in past 12 to 18 months

High team attrition

Higher than average % of low performers

New hire ramp rate lower than average

Not completing manager training

Reps not completing mandatory or other training

Low frequency of 1:1s, coaching sessions

Low team engagement scores

Low leadership trust scores

"Great," said Chloe. "Let's talk now about managers. We'll create a predictive model to identify managers with profiles similar to those who lose team members. Same analytics as for reps."

"Are we sure we want to keep managers like these around?" questioned Bobby, pointing to the screen and raising an eyebrow.

"The thinking," Martha answered, "is that, like the underperforming reps, it's better to give them a chance to turn things around than to have to fill yet more open roles. Besides, we promoted them without the right skills and then didn't insist they take the right training, so in a sense we owe it to them. And some of them might go back to being great reps if given the chance."

Bobby sighed and leaned back in his chair. "I'm not a big fan of being wrong, people. Can you fix it so that I can start being right and telling other people *they're* wrong? Like, really soon?"

"We're doing our best, Bobby," replied Marcus, smiling. "I promise. Chloe, tell Bobby all about the prescriptive analytics."

"Glad to," Chloe replied. "Once we know who's at risk, we can *prescribe* interventions. For example, since we know the top revenue-driving KPIs, we can train low producers who are struggling in those areas and train managers on how to better coach to those KPIs. Martha suspects that assigning each rep a buddy will work, too. She may be right, but we'll have to test that theory."

Martha nodded, clearly enthusiastic.

"Normally," continued Chloe, "we'd do that with 'A/B testing'—use interventions on one group and compare their results to a control group that didn't receive support. But we have an urgent situation, so we'll give everyone support and track outcomes closely. Eventually, as we collect more data, we'll be able to assess and prescribe the enablement most correlated to driving sustainable growth."

"But in some cases, interventions don't require fancy analytics," added Marcus. "For example, we suggest Sales leaders conduct 'stay interviews' with high producers to determine what will keep them here. Those conversations would be guided by what we learned in exit interviews and surveys about what's driving away similar reps. "

"Sounds good to me. But what about those new managers who are driving away reps?" Bobby asked. "Let's fix that situation, *stat*."

"My team is urgently redesigning a new manager development course that's mandatory," Martha reported, "including effective hiring, on-boarding, and coaching. Based on that, we'll tweak existing sales leadership development programming."

"Don't take this question the wrong way," said Bobby cautiously, "but what are the concrete objectives here?"

"Bobby, you challenged us to cut rep attrition by 50 percent, and that's what we intend to do," answered Pam. "That was my directive to Chloe, and I'm confident that she and the team are driving toward that."

"Fantastic. Now how about you explain how we're gonna fill our open spots in record time?" Bobby asked, friendly but firm in his request.

"Great segue to our Talent Acquisition initiative," declared Chloe. "As I mentioned earlier, we can better attract, screen, and interview candidates based on sales rep DNA, together with increasing the likelihood of accepting our offer. All that should significantly shorten the time to hire. Here's the idea in a nutshell."

IMPROVE
HIRING PROCESS

Right hiring criteria

Right interview questions

Right candidate evaluation and scoring

Right talent targeting (longer term)

"To start," Chloe continued, "we'll use the sales rep DNA to develop an ideal candidate profile, job description, and hiring criteria. We can also do résumé screening. It's a pretty new field so I recommend we outsource a résumé screening solution. It'll analyze our résumé database to learn which candidates become successful employees based on factors like performance and tenure, and then assess job candidates based on those factors, extracting résumé data through text-mining and natural language processing technology. Newer hiring software packages actually include résumé screening."

"Explain the part about likelihood to accept the offer—that's the best part," enthused Elke.

"Right!" exclaimed Chloe. "We can predict, with decent accuracy, a candidate's likelihood of accepting an offer based on two inputs. The 'job readiness score' indicates their skills, experience, and profile vis-à-vis the role. The 'propensity to accept score' is based on the anticipated attractiveness of the role, like title and salary versus current role, and their job search activity, tracked on LinkedIn by their level of networking, connecting with recruiters, and so forth. These indicate how serious they are about looking for new work."

"Could we track our reps' job search activity as another way to predict which ones might fly the coop?" asked Bobby.

"We could," answered Chloe, "but the sales rep DNA gives us so many insights that it's not really necessary. Some companies go even further to predict employee behavior, using sentiment analysis software to mine emails, chats, and blogs for clues about their engagement, likelihood to leave, and so on. It's legal here in the United States, but somewhat controversial. Some people find it creepy."

"There's definitely a 'creepy factor,'" added Pam. "Let's be sure we'd feel 100 percent comfortable sharing our analytics initiatives with employees. Looking at LinkedIn data is different, in my view, because it's publicly available, and it's now a fairly standard HR practice. We haven't decided yet whether we'll start analyzing that data for our employees, though, so stay tuned. Chloe, anything more on hiring?"

"A few last things, "she replied. "A simpler use of diagnostics is to yield interview guidelines. For example, we learned through descriptive analytics that the average deal size of our most successful reps is $250k. So we'll want hiring managers to ask about deal size experience. Using all of this input, we'll update the candidate scoring system."

Chloe took a breath before continuing: "Listen, guys, data analytics is very powerful, but it isn't a panacea. Machines can pinpoint interview questions, but there's no substitute for an effective interviewer who can read people well. And no algorithm is ever perfect. By using any of the methods I've been describing we may miss candidates who would have been selected by an actual person. There are major benefits and some costs to consider."

"That's a very important point," said Pam, "and a message we'll need to repeat to various partners and stakeholders. Let's under-promise and over-deliver."

"Bobby, I'm very optimistic about how this will drive improvements for your team, bearing in mind Chloe's caveats, of course," Elke enthused. "And longer term, we can use all this data for talent marketing, so we can proactively build our candidate pipeline by reaching out to the right candidates on LinkedIn and elsewhere, even if they haven't applied yet."

"I'm impressed," said Bobby, "but I have to ask again: What objectives are we working toward?"

Elke jumped in. "Chloe and I feel that within the next two months we can reduce average time to hire from twelve weeks to eight weeks, and double the high-quality candidate acceptance rate, from 20 percent to 40 percent. We're expecting even better numbers long term, returning at least to industry benchmarks. Anne and I formed a joint working group from our teams to develop a new innovation-based employer brand and social media recruitment marketing campaign."

"Bobby, how does that sit with you?" asked Pam.

"Like a tick on a fat dog!" quipped Bobby.

"Terrific," said Pam, smiling. "Team, great work. And I know you're not just working with Chloe on these analytics projects. What other actions are we taking?"

Sameer answered first. "We've got some exciting projects ahead. I'll be preparing my employee contact center staff to answer questions, especially from sales reps and managers. I'll also work with Chloe to streamline reporting processes and derive more insight from our data, and to change our KPIs from efficiency-focused to impact-focused. We'll start by replacing 'call time' with 'caller satisfaction.' And we will integrate all the data sources Chloe tapped to understand the sales rep attrition ecosystem—internal data like exit inter-views and external data such as Glassdoor. By integrating it all, we can do more complex analytics and solve or even prevent issues down the road."

"My team are I are supporting Chloe with business insights and any support she may need regarding additional data," said Marcus. "I'm also enabling my team to help engage with leaders to prepare them for the changes to come and to follow up with Marketing and Product to track progress on their initiatives, which you mentioned at the beginning of this meeting, Pam. We're also focusing on who else from the busi-ness should be involved in the new change management task force that David just announced," he concluded.

"Guess I'm right on time," said Exalted CEO David Craig, strolling into the room. Pam and Bobby rose to shake his hand as the team members looked at each other with a mix of surprise and pride.

"Thanks for joining us, David," said Pam. "Glad you could spare a few minutes to see what my team has planned. Chloe has put together an executive summary for you that I'll for-ward later today. We've just wrapped up analytics planning and are discussing related initiatives."

"Thanks, Pam," David replied. "Sounds like you've all done a bang-up job. I didn't mean to interrupt. Please go on."

"I'm happy to go next," said Martha, "Longer term, we'll train all reps on key success drivers. And we'll get down to work on really responding to engagement survey results, now that you have shown your support for that, David."

"Absolutely," replied the CEO. "Thanks to you and Pam, I understand just how sanitized survey results had been in the past. We've got to have transparency and accountability. It will help Exalted leaders to walk the talk about using data instead of just intuition to solve problems. It's also about time we listened to our employees."

"But the real reason I came by," David continued, "is the new change management task force Marcus mentioned. Pam, I'd like you to head up that effort and ensure that data driven decision making is at the core of how we change as a company."

All eyes were on Pam.

"I'd be honored, David," she replied, to the applause of her team. Bobby clapped and whistled loudly.

The meeting concluded on that high note. As the group dispersed, Bobby took Pam aside. "I didn't want to say anything in front of your team, but I was surprised to hear that Anne is on board. Isn't Ashcroft giving her a hard time?"

"He is," Pam replied, "but she feels she can't ignore the evidence, plus David and the whole leadership team are behind the changes, so she can't ignore them either. After our weekly squash game yesterday, she told me it's a big strain on their relationship. But she plans to hold firm."

"Well," Bobby responded, "let's just hope that the winds of change will either sweep Tom Ashcroft along with us in the right direction—or boot that Yankee straight out the door."

With one last wink, he turned and walked away.

SUMMARY

It's been two weeks since Chloe presented her findings on the sales rep attrition ecosystem, and a week since she and the Exalted HR Leadership Team spent two days brainstorming with Sales Operations leaders on how to move forward. Chloe, Elke, Marcus, Martha, and Sameer reconvene to share with Pam their analytics action plan, explaining their process and anticipated results, and prioritizing key turnaround factors: stem sales rep departures, especially among top sellers; train reps and managers; and improve hiring processes. They're joined by CSO Bobby Cash, who asks important clarifying questions about the value of analytics and concrete goals for their action plan. CEO David Craig appears, asking Pam to head Exalted's new change management task force. Pam confides to Bobby that, although Ashcroft is pressuring CMO Anne Rodriguez, she plans to support the company's new direction.

COMMENTARY

BRINGING ALLIES ALONG ON THE JOURNEY

Pam and the team are at a key stage in their journey: developing solutions for issues that have been identified. Continuing to enlist allies and make the project inclusive, Pam was smart to include Sales Operations in the brainstorming off-site led by Chloe and in the action plan that followed, as her team could only be successful helping sales reps and managers with the insights and involvement of sales colleagues. Yet she also wisely stays out of areas that are not within the HR purview, such as pricing and product development.

While Bobby has been increasingly supportive, Pam and Chloe both know that to get his full backing, they'll need to respect that he is new to this analytics rodeo and understand that his questions don't reflect antagonism but rather an honest lack of awareness. Never underestimate the value of patience nor the ability to educate stakeholders without talking down to them. This is true for any new initiative, but especially analytics, as not all senior leaders will be as willing as Bobby to admit not having all the answers.

One of Bobby's queries may come up in your conversations as well. Someone knowledgeable in a business discipline, but not analytics, may question whether early findings aren't "obvious." Follow Chloe's example and take the time to walk that person through all the reasons why analytics can uncover insights that would be difficult or impossible to ascertain through intuition only. Reality is often much more complex than what might seem obvious at first. Without analytics, Pam and the team might never have learned why top reps were leaving or even that certain managers were more likely to lose team members than others.

Another key advantage to using analytics is the ability to get to the root of a problem rather than to ignore it or to deal with symptoms. Pam and the team have clearly identified reps who aren't good at selling and managers who aren't good at leading. Lesser leaders might simply fire them, but Pam and Bobby do not. While it can be tempting to remove weak players quickly, it's far better to understand and address what's causing them to under-perform and then help them with targeted interventions. Analytics makes that possible.

IF IT MATTERS, PROVIDE TRAINING AND TRACK SUCCESS—USING DATA

While hiring is among a manager's most important roles, too many organizations fail to train managers in select-ing quality candidates likely to become productive quickly, succeed in their roles, perform at a high level, stay with the company, and so on. Even fewer track manager effective-ness in these areas.

Imagine how your organization might avoid these mis-takes, taking a page from the Exalted playbook and using analytics:

- Identify the managers best at hiring employees who suc-ceed in their roles (see above), using HR hiring and per-formance data.
- Understand these managers' common traits and behav-iors, using HR, performance, and LMS data (namely, whether they've completed training on hiring).
- Interview these managers on how they approach hiring.
- Leverage all inputs to improve (or create) hiring training, targeting first those managers *worst* at hiring.
- Measure improvements in hiring, retention, performance, and other analytics, calculating ROI if possible and, of course, reporting results to senior leadership,
- Refine approaches based on findings.

Identifying what makes employees successful and how managers can better assess these qualities is key to hiring more productive employees. This is just one example of how Human Resources can accelerate business performance. People are a company's single biggest competitive advantage, and we are responsible for the people. We can and must do more to ensure strategic success for our organizations.

BE COOL, NOT CREEPY

This is critically important advice. Sentiment analysis, which comes up in this chapter, uses unstructured data to identify attitudes, such as like/dislike and others. Interpreting people's words can get sticky in consumer uses, where sentiment analysis originated, and even more so for HR.

The "creepy" factor is real; endeavor to avoid it. Be sensitive to the difference, for example, between analyzing employee comments that are openly shared via internal social media platforms and analyzing the content of employee emails, which feels innately invasive,[1] even if your company is legally permitted to access correspondence on its servers.

Also, stay tuned into shifts in norms. A paper from Accenture observes that what's cool and what's creepy is a matter of general cultural acceptance and evolves over time; after all, in the 1990s, caller ID was considered Orwellian.[2] Accenture provides one piece of advice to retailers that can easily transfer to the corporate domain. Simply substitute "employees" for "customers": "Understand where you stand and actively work on your relationship. Be conscious of how much customers trust your company and take deliberate steps to increase their trust."

APPLYING PREDICTIVE ANALYTICS TO IMPROVE SALES REP PERFORMANCE

In Chapter 2, Exalted CSO Bobby Cash rejects analytics outright, favoring his own intuition. In Chapter 6, as discussed above, Bobby has evolved but still questions whether analytical findings aren't obvious. Nothing should be taken for granted as obvious—certainly not when analytics are available to guide us. Here are some examples of how predictive analytics can improve sales performance: hiring the right people, training them in the right performance areas, enabling them with the right tools and knowledge, managing them well, and giving them opportunities to grow, while helping non-performers find more suitable employment (see Figure 6c.1).

This is only a partial list, but it illustrates the point that choosing which levers to pull (that is, which KPIs or variables to strengthen) is not a simple task. Without some sort of guidance, you can waste a lot of time and energy trying to address every issue from hiring to exiting. Data analytics can pinpoint the major problem areas and the variables that provide the biggest leverage for change, so you can apply corrective actions judiciously and strategically instead of blindly and broadly.

We invite you to use this chart as a model or foundation for other parts of your business as well, extrapolating from the guidelines provided on the following page and throughout *The Data Driven Leader*.

Sales Rep Lifecycle

Hire/ Onboard Them	Train Them	Enable Them	Manage and Motivate Them	Grow/ Exit Them

Application of Predictive Analytics

Hire/ Onboard Them	Train Them	Enable Them	Manage and Motivate Them	Grow/ Exit Them
Which candidates are most likely to perform?	Which employees need training intervention?	Which prospects are highly likely to buy?	Which sales person is likely to miss quota?	Which salesperson is likely to leave?
Which candidates are most likely to be high potential?	Which training are they most likely to benefit from?	What are the prospects most likely to buy?	What are the top competency issues?	Which retention strategy is most likely to work?
Which candidates are a good fit for succession?	What is the likely impact of each of the training courses?	How much are they likely to spend at what price?	Which manager is most likely to perform?	Which reps have little future potential, and which should be exited?
Which candidates are fit for certain role types?		Who are they likely to buy from?	Which partner is most likely to perform?	Which candidates should be promoted as managers?
		When are they likely to buy?	Which sales channel is most likely to perform?	
		Which deals are most likely to close?	Predict quota attainment?	

Figure 6c.1. Sales Rep Lifecycle

173

NOTES

1. Kaveh Waddell, "The Algorithms That Tell Bosses How Employees Are Feeling," *The Atlantic*, September 29, 2016, accessed May 25, 2017, https://www.theatlantic.com/technology/archive/2016/09/the-algorithms-that-tell-bosses-how-employees-feel/502064/.

2. Accenture Labs, *Retail Hyperpersonalization: Creepy or Cool?* Accenture, last updated 2015, accessed May 25, 2017, https://www.accenture.com/t20160728T163156__w__/ca-en/_acnmedia/Accenture/Conversion-Assets/DotCom/Documents/Global/PDF/Dualpub_8/Accenture-Technology-Labs-Hyperpersonalization.pdf.

Chapter 7

RESULTS WIN SUPPORT

JUST OVER NINE MONTHS LATER . . . JANUARY 15

CHRO Pam Sharp was ready. Her laptop was connected to the projector, her presentation printed out for her reference with a few handwritten notes, and she'd prepared her remarks with her usual meticulous attention to detail and outcomes. She'd also reviewed the content of her slides with CEO David Craig, who had been pleased. She had rehearsed with CSO Bobby Cash, CMO Anne Rodriguez, and other C-level leaders who'd been involved in data analytics initiatives to one extent or another since the previous March. She was confident that potential objections were addressable.

The first Exalted Enterprises board meeting of the new year felt momentous, but not as high-stakes as it had seemed nine months before, when Pam was confident but not yet assured that her analytics projects would triumph.

Eventually, all the attendees arrived and took seats around the large oval boardroom table and, after a few opening items over which the board president presided, it was Pam's moment of truth. David nodded at her with that same look of confidence he had shown at their dinner meeting more than a year earlier. Now he was even more certain he'd made the right choice. Anne gave a quick thumbs-up, and Bobby winked, elbowing Chloe, seated beside him. Thomas Ashcroft sat on the opposite end of the room, tight-lipped, serious, and oblivious to all this silent bonding.

Pam rose and walked to the lectern.

"Good morning, everyone," she began confidently. "Thank you for this opportunity to share the phenomenal progress

176

achieved at Exalted Enterprises since our team formed last February. I'd like to follow up on the quarterly updates I've been sharing with you since April and deliver the year-end report."

She advanced to her first slide.

"I'm sure you all recognize these figures," she continued, "our key performance indicators when I joined Exalted nearly a year ago. I'm very proud to present to you on this next slide the year-end results, which reflect a very different reality for our company."

Pam went on, "We've improved every major health indicator for our company and are well on our way to healthy profitability, which is expected within two quarters. As you can see, our newer products are leading the recovery, growing a stellar 25 percent in revenue booking."

Advancing to the next slide, the CHRO continued, "Another key set of data to share is on engagement, an often-underappreciated metric. Research consistently finds positive correlations between engaged employees and company financials. We are seeing this play out at Exalted, as well."

"I think we've heard enough of this," Thomas Ashcroft suddenly interrupted, his voice calm but clearly antagonistic. "It looks to me like you're trying to pull the wool over everyone's eyes, Ms. Sharp. But your numbers aren't believable. I want to know where you got your data and I want to see the math. And engagement drives *revenue*? Do you expect any of us to buy that?"

Pam responded calmly to the irate board member. Having anticipated the range of his potential objections, she was

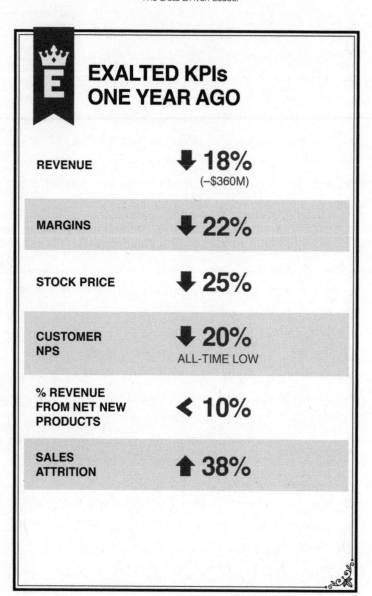

EXALTED YEAR-END RESULTS

REVENUE	⬇ 18% (−$360M)	⬆ 12% (25% NEW PRODUCTS)
MARGINS	⬇ 22%	⬆ 20%
STOCK PRICE	⬇ 25%	⬆ 30%
CUSTOMER NPS	⬇ 20% ALL-TIME LOW	⬆ 10%
% REVENUE FROM NET NEW PRODUCTS	❮ 10%	❯ 40%
SALES ATTRITION	⬆ 38%	⬇ 50% (TOP, MID-LEVEL SELLERS)
ENGAGEMENT		⬆ 10%

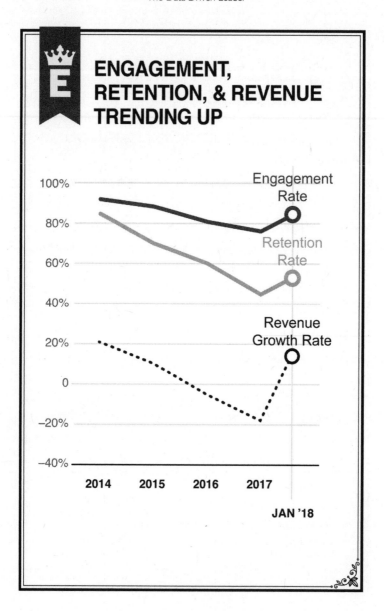

ready. "The numbers came from our CFO, Sales, and other internal groups. They've been confirmed and validated by senior leadership, including David. They're not HR's numbers; these are *our corporate* numbers."

"Well, even if they're true, they're not sustainable," Ashcroft retorted. "Your little analytics game was a one-time win. There were clearly other factors at work. Exalted is simply riding a market trend—the rising tide raises all boats. I just read two analyst reports that said exactly that. Once people realize these new products are nothing more than a trend, we'll be right back in the top position, and as the *premium* provider, selling what we've always sold. Engagement! Ha! This isn't about your HR analytics."

Bobby Cash raised a hand and interjected, "You're right, Tom, it's not just the analytics. But from what my reps tell me they hear from our customers, this isn't a trend. It's the future. We're on board, and we're already seeing results. We're thinking differently about how we hire, how we train our managers, how we coach and incent our reps. We were bleeding sales reps nine months ago, which was a huge burn of time and resources, not to mention stupidly expensive in terms of lost revenue opportunities. Now our attrition numbers are nearly at industry benchmarks, and my people are working as a team again. To be honest, I was just as suspicious as you, but the results won me over."

"I should have expected you sales types to stick together," Ashcroft sneered, "and to ignore actual industry experts. A few positive financials and everyone oohs and aahs and ignores reality. Anne, we've talked about this many times. Surely *you* have come to your senses!"

CMO Anne Rodriguez looked profoundly uncomfortable, shifting in her chair as the tension in the room grew. Pam was suddenly unsure whether Anne would be able to contradict her mentor in front of the Exalted executive leadership and board. In their planning, neither had anticipated just how stubbornly Tom Ashcroft would stand against validated corporate results.

Then Anne composed herself and began to answer. "Tom, you and everyone here know how much I respect you and how grateful I am for your support and guidance. It's your guidance that kept Exalted leading the market for so long, so we are all grateful to you. Market dynamics are simply forcing us to think differently about how we price products and position them. I couldn't ignore the numbers, and with Pam's help have been able to identify sustainable changes that have positively impacted the business. We needed a fresh set of eyes and perspective to take us to the next level. But if you hadn't gotten us as far as you did, we couldn't have taken this next step. We actually owe this success to you."

Ashcroft leaned forward as if he were going to respond, and then, clearly changing his mind, leaned back in his seat and simply gave a quick nod in Anne's direction. The conference room was completely still.

Then the CEO broke the silence. "The increase in revenue alone has made the entire analytics effort worth the investment," David said confidently. "To me, it's clear that

Pam has proven that data analytics are fundamental to our business success. Data driven decision making and leadership are essential to our future, to ensure that we not only survive but thrive in a new market reality. Toward that end, I am very pleased to announce a new centralized organization called Enterprise Analytics."

"This group," he continued, "will design structures and methodologies across the company to drive analytics capacity in each of the business units, which can build expertise over time and go deeper on function-specific analysis. Enterprise Analytics will work hand in hand with our change management team to start shaping a data driven culture at Exalted, not just among leaders but among all employees. Tom, do you have any questions or objections?"

"None," said Ashcroft, as casually as he could, seemingly preoccupied by brushing lint off the sleeve of his navy wool blazer.

"Pam, I think the board is interested in hearing just how analytics played a role in turning around our financials and other key metrics. Will you walk us through it?"

"I'd be happy to, David," Pam replied. "That was next on my list. Here is the Sales Rep Attrition Ecosystem slide that should now be familiar to you from previous board meetings. As you know, last March, we discovered through data analytics eight key factors impacting sales rep attrition, which was as high as 60 percent for our top producers."

"What we discovered in putting together the pieces of the puzzle," she said, going on to the next slide, "was the story you now know."

SALES REP
ATTRITION ECOSYSTEM

COMPENSATION QUOTA
ATTAINMENT

PRODUCT MANAGERS

**SALES REP
ATTRITION
ECOSYSTEM**

PRICE

ENABLEMENT

ENGAGEMENT HIRING

SALES REP ATTRITION ECOSYSTEM
What Caused Our Top Reps to Leave?

○ **COMPENSATION**	Incented sales of unpopular, older products
○ **QUOTA ATTAINMENT**	Unrealistically high, cut top rep commissions
○ **MANAGERS**	Inexperienced/ untrained, drove away teams
○ **ENABLEMENT**	Optional; not focused on key revenue drivers
○ **HIRING**	Quantity-over-quality screening, top picks rejected offers
○ **ENGAGEMENT**	Above issues + poor change management hurt morale
○ **PRICE**	Strategy shift not well-communicated/ executed
○ **PRODUCT**	Underestimated market desire for new products

"Exalted, once the market leader, couldn't innovate fast enough to adapt to a rapidly shifting marketplace, so we acquired new products," Pam summarized. "But like many companies before us, and surely many others to come, we underestimated the change management component required to communicate, gain buy-in, and operationalize such a fundamental shift in our business model. Many, but not all, of Exalted's problems radiated outward from this underestimation. I've shown you this slide before, so I'll move on to the analytics initiatives that, as you've seen, have yielded substantial results for our company."

Pam summarized each item for the board, as Bobby, Anne, and others inserted color commentary, especially regarding deviations from initial plans or surprising results. For example, Bobby explained how their overall strategy had evolved. Not only had they reduced quota expectations for top producers to better match territory potential, but they'd also hired more top performers, which helped relieve psychological *and* sales pressure while boosting revenue.

They had also discovered a few months into their plan that special coaching and training could bolster mid-level reps' skills and success, which gave sales an important boost. They learned that, although some bottom reps performed better with additional coaching and development, those who didn't improve after reasonable effort were unlikely to do so. Managing these reps out with compassion led to several positive outcomes: it freed up managers to provide more coaching, which lifted results for mid- and top-performing reps; and it

SALES REP ATTRITION ECOSYSTEM
How Are We Keeping (and Attracting) Top Reps?

○ **COMPENSATION** (Sales) — New incentives aligned with strategy

○ **QUOTA** (Sales) — Recalibrated quotas to achievable levels

○ **MANAGERS** (L+D & Sales) — Urgent + ongoing training

○ **ENABLEMENT** (L+D & Sales) — Training/coaching on top revenue drivers

○ **HIRING** (Talent Acq. & Sales) — Ideal sales rep DNA-driven screening, interviewing, etc.

○ **ENGAGEMENT** (Sales + L&D) — Comp, quota, training fixes; "stay interviews"

○ **PRICE** (Marketing) — Revamp corporate and employer brand strategy, tactics

○ **PRODUCT** (Products) — Ramping up dev, acquisition, portfolio integration opened up positions for new top sales talent. That coincided with the new analytics-driven Talent Acquisition processes being implemented, and hiring improved significantly. Within months, Exalted once again had a robust talent pipeline.

Pam also provided quick updates on additional efforts, such as the success of Sameer's HR Global Shared Services team in integrating all the internal and external data sources they had tapped to understand the sales rep attrition ecosystem. In fact, GSS had provided a blueprint to the new Enterprise Analytics group on database integration and was providing technical support as the new group got off the ground.

Finally, Pam summarized the achievements of the change management task force. It was a combined effort, she explained, centered around the new company strategy and a carefully designed data driven culture, where analytics would play a central role for all employees, especially leaders. Accordingly, they updated Exalted's company values, behaviors, and employee value proposition; revamped their engagement survey, including full transparency and team accountability plans in response to results; multi-faceted employee communications; and comprehensive company-wide operationalization plans. Together, the task force had raised awareness of the new strategy and priorities from 20 percent at baseline measurement in May to nearly 80 percent in mid-December.

David Craig thanked his CHRO for her exceptional contributions to the company and, after a few additional agenda items, the meeting adjourned. Tom Ashcroft approached David as he was returning papers to his briefcase.

"David, I've enjoyed my time at Exalted, but it's clear that you don't need my services anymore," Ashcroft said, betraying no emotions. "I'll be sending you my letter of resignation in the morning."

Before the CEO could reply, Ashcroft held up his hand. "Let's keep this professional, no hard feelings," he pronounced with a tight smile, grabbed his overcoat and briefcase, and strode out of the room.

Pam caught David's eye from across the board room. He gave her a discrete smile and turned to the board chair, who enthusiastically shook his hand and leaned in close to start a conversation that Pam was too far away to overhear. She instead turned to her colleagues, who showered her with congratulations and ushered her out of the room for a celebratory dinner.

A FEW DAYS LATER . . .

Pam knocked on the office door before entering. David Craig looked up from his desk and motioned for her to enter. After Pam had taken a seat and the two exchanged their insights about the current NBA season, David spoke.

"Pam, your performance at the meeting did not go unnoticed," he began. "The board, now minus Ashcroft, has big expectations for you and your future at Exalted. When you and I met about bringing you here, one thing I didn't mention is that I've been planning to retire early. I've been working hard my whole life, and I've earned the right to spend time with my grandchildren and take my wife sailing around the world. I've been looking for the right person to take my place in the next few years, and I can't think of anyone more qualified or better positioned to ensure Exalted's future success than you."

Pam smiled. "David, I've never backed down from a challenge, and I'm not about to start now. Besides, you persuaded me to move to Chicago in January and that has worked out pretty well, so I know that you're all about taking the right risks. Count me in."

"Great," David answered. "Then mark your calendar for a week from Thursday. The Warriors are back in town to play the Bulls, and I've arranged for you and your team to have one heck of a celebration at our United Center corporate suite."

Pam thanked him for his support and confidence and promised to deliver continued successes. After they discussed a few details and shook hands, Pam walked out the door and down the hallway, leaping to toss an imaginary basketball through an unseen net. She landed squarely on her feet, smoothed her skirt, and continued on her way, already planning for the banner year she was certain lay ahead.

SUMMARY

A little more than nine months after the team presented its analytics plan, Pam Sharp summarizes for the Exalted Board of Directors the turnaround that the company has undergone thanks to data analytics. While the numbers are very positive and compelling, Thomas Ashcroft will have none of it. Fully prepared, Pam gets support from David, Bobby, and even Anne, who tries to soften the blow for Ashcroft. Still, in the face of total opposition to his point of view, he is silenced. Pam walks the board through the issues they uncovered and how they solved them and presents the accomplishments of the change management task force she headed. At the end of the meeting, Ashcroft resigns from the board.

A few days later, David reveals his succession plan: Pam will take over as CEO when he takes early retirement. Pam accepts.

COMMENTARY

PRESENTING (AKA DEFENDING) YOUR RESULTS

In this final chapter, Pam faces the scrutiny of Exalted's Board of Directors. While your analytics project may not need approval from a board, many of the same principles apply regardless of the leaders to whom you will undoubtedly be presenting.

Keep it simple. Remember that your audience is likely not as versed in the details as you are and may not understand or accept what seem like logical and sound conclusions. It fact, you may encounter strong resistance, especially from those who may advocate a different solution or feel their positions or expertise have been challenged.

Be prepared. That's why it's key to have prepared solid results that demonstrate knowledge of the organizational issues to be addressed and defendable data analytics to back up assumptions and conclusions. Even if you are not as fortunate as Pam to know who will oppose you and are blindsided in a meeting, you will be in a much better position to explain and defend your findings. Data is more powerful than opinions, as Pam's interactions with Ashcroft reflect.

Prepare others. Another key part of preparation involves your allies and leaders. Never surprise your executive team in front of the board. Pam has carefully and thoroughly briefed and prepared David, Bobby, and Anne, as she needs them on her side, especially knowing Ashcroft will have objections. Colleagues may be key to disarming skeptics who persist despite your thorough analysis.

Speak the language of business. Pam is careful to remind the board of the business needs that drove her initiative. This ensures everyone is on the same page and primes them to see the impact on bottom-line organizational metrics. Too often, Human Resources leaders talk about "soft" metrics like retention and engagement, which are not nearly as compelling to business leaders—especially a board—as revenue, profitability, customer satisfaction, and stock price. When Pam does discuss engagement, she doesn't discuss whether employees are happy, but rather shows the correlation of engagement with retention and revenue.

While the work of Pam and her team is fiction, the examples used throughout this book are based on actual business situations. It may seem impossible to obtain the level of results that Pam and her team achieved in the narrative, but a carefully designed and executed analytics project can yield similar results in your organization. While we have presented a fairly complex set of business issues, it may be wise to start small, gain some early wins, and build on the momentum.

STARTING TO BUILD YOUR ANALYTICS CAPABILITY

LEADERSHIP IS KEY

Data analytics is most valuable when it is viewed not simply as a tool to solve problems, but as a mindset to increase overall effectiveness. This mindset needs to be translated into a solid plan supported by adequate resources, staffed by competent personnel, and led by a transformational leader.

The leader of a data analytics initiative can be from Sales, Marketing, Sales, Operations, Learning & Development, Human Resources, IT, or somewhere else in the company, but must have credibility, influence, and a reputation for success. When the initiative impacts the whole organization or a large percentage of it, the CEO, president, or COO may be the best overall leader.

STAFFING UP

As you build up in-house data analytics capabilities and adopt a data driven decision making approach, realize that it may not be easy to hire well-trained people to staff your initiative. Talent remains a critical constraint to realizing data analytics' full potential, with a current estimated

U.S. labor force shortfall of 250,000 data scientists—a 25 percent increase since 2011—and projected demand for between two and four million data-savvy business leaders who can translate between the C-suite and the data lab. And, buyer beware, this rising demand for data scientists, ranked the number one job in 2016 by Glassdoor.com, has led their average salaries to rise eight times as fast as general wages from 2012 to 2014.[1]

Be aware, too, that you may need not just a "data scientist"—for which demand is forecast to increase by 28 percent by 2020—but one of a range of professional roles within data science and analytics, such as data engineering and data visualization, and specializations like data privacy and security and data governance.[2]

Thus, a key first question is whether to engage the services of consultants and, if so, when. Begin by identifying the skill gaps on your team so you can bring in the right solution to solve specific problems. Pam brings in Chloe because she needs an analytics expert, but she doesn't immediately hire a consulting firm because she wants to keep the initiative lean and focused and because she has prior experience implementing an analytics program.

If one or more people at your company have strong data analytics skills and experience, you may be able to start your initiative without external consultants. You'll need to carefully assess your needs. If they are significant, a consulting firm could help with both planning and execution. However, bringing in too much consulting power too fast can create confusion and rob your people of the opportunity to take ownership and grow; worse yet, it can potentially sabotage the whole initiative if the board sees it as an expensive boondoggle.

GUIDELINES AND FIRST STEPS

Giving you detailed step-by-step instructions on how to build your data analytics capability is beyond the scope of this book, but here are some rules of thumb to start:

- **Don't rely solely on software.** Resist the urge to rush out and buy analytics software, which will do you no good unless you have people who know how to use it and a back end that can supply the right data.
- **Get the right expertise.** If you hire a data analytics expert, bring in one who understands both business and technology and can help solve your problems, not simply help you with the technical aspects of analytics. Ideally, that person will also have HR experience.
- **Request recommendations from trustworthy people, but interview carefully.** The same consultant won't work for everyone.
- **Educate yourself.** Learn enough about data analytics to be able to ask the right questions. Even if you are not technically minded, you can gain considerable understanding by reading articles and books like this one.

CENTRALIZED OR DECENTRALIZED?

Should you build your own internal HR analytics practice or join a company-wide team? In this book, Exalted creates a centralized Enterprise Analytics group, although there can be advantages to going your own way, especially if no organizational initiative yet exists.

In *Creating a Data-Driven Organization: Practical Advice from the Trenches*, author Carl Anderson weighs each approach.[3] The advantages to a centralized analytics team, selected by two-thirds of more analytically mature organizations, include standardization of skills, training, and tools used, efficiencies of shared software and other resources, and enhanced ease in promoting the use of data analytics on an organization-wide basis. Decentralization, he cautions, may lead to a duplication of efforts and problems with interoperability and diluted cultural clout, but can benefit from faster turnaround times, direct access to analytics at a team- or division-level, and less bureaucracy.

COMMUNICATIONS AND TRUST

Prior to introducing analytics initiatives, leadership should discuss ethical considerations and openly communicate their policies and commitments to employees who demonstrate awareness of these issues and respect for individual privacy. Make clear that the goal is to improve employee and company success, not to punish or embarrass people who are doing poorly.

Ultimately, employees want their efforts to be successful; they want to be on a winning team and will likely embrace a data analytics initiative that helps them attain these goals, if communicated and administered with transparency and respect.

JUST DO IT!

A successful data analytics program will help your people perform better, which in turn will make your company more successful. Success attracts success, and top performers attract top performers. It's a self-perpetuating upward spiral.

You, too, can see remarkable impact for your organization.

NOTES

1. Nicolaus Henke, Jacques Bughin, Michael Chui, James Manyika, Tamim Saleh, Bill Wiseman, and Guru Sethupathy, *The Age of Analytics: Competing in a Data-Driven World* (New York: McKinsey Global Institute, December 2016), 38–40, accessed May 25, 2017, http://www.mckinsey.com/business-functions/mckinsey-analytics/our-insights/the-age-of-analytics-competing-in-a-data-driven-world.

2. Steven Miller and Debbie Hughes, *The Quant Crunch: How the Demand for Data Science Skills Is Disrupting the Job Market* (Boston, MA: Burning Glass Technologies, 2017), 6, accessed May 25, 2017, https://www-01.ibm.com/common/ssi/cgi-bin/ssialias?htmlfid=IML14576USEN.

3. Carl Anderson, *Creating a Data-Driven Organization: Practical Advice from the Trenches* (Sebastopol, CA: O'Reilly, 2015), 77–79, accessed May 25, 2017, https://books.google.com/books?id=MVpDCgAAQBAJ&pg=PA78&lpg=PA78.

ESSENTIAL READING

This section will provide you with fundamental insights to guide your HR analytics efforts:

1. The Four Stages of Analytics—a helpful summary of the types of analytics your initiatives will encompass
2. HR Analytics Review—key concepts, metrics, and analytics use case examples in core areas of human capital management (Leadership Development and Succession Management, Learning Management, Performance Management, Talent Acquisition, and Total Rewards)

THE FOUR STAGES OF ANALYTICS

As summarized in the Chapter 3 Commentary, data analytics is commonly categorized as descriptive, diagnostic, predictive, or prescriptive. Below are additional explanations and insights on each of these four stages.

1. Descriptive Analytics

Explanation: Descriptive analytics is a process of discovery that answers the question "What happened?" by means of reports and dashboards. Although this is the first and least technologically sophisticated of the four levels, it is still very powerful. As we saw in Chapter 4, descriptive findings led Chloe toward deeper discoveries. But you'll likely still need to answer *why* the data says what it does and which variables are most influential, requiring more advanced analytics that employ statistical algorithms.

Example: Chloe's chart in Chapter 4 titled "Top Producers Have Unattainable Quotas" is a great example of the compelling insights descriptive analytics can surface. Chloe developed this report by persistent, intelligent exploration. She started by investigating *why* there's high attrition among top sales reps. The next logical question was: What's special about the ones who are leaving? To answer the question, Chloe looked at attrition versus many available KPIs, including bookings, which revealed that top producers had the highest attrition, and the lowest commissions. This was curious, so she continued to investigate to understand *why* this was so.

She discovers that the quotas for top reps were set too high. Even though she unearthed the answer through descriptive techniques, we can call the result diagnostic because it answers the crucial "why" question. The definition of diagnostic analytics is slippery—it can be as simple as making charts of KPIs, or as complex as fitting predictive models.

Descriptive analytics can also be an unpredictable process, as not every question yields an interesting answer. If Chloe had found that the relationship between quota and bookings was similar for all sales reps, further thinking and exploring would have been required. It is possible to construct millions of charts from all the data available, but only a small fraction of them will be interesting or informative, and an even smaller fraction will be meaningful in a business sense.

Insight: A common pitfall of descriptive analytics is selection bias. If you have some hypothesis about what's going on in your business, you could almost certainly come up with five charts that support your hypothesis. Yet it's often possible to come up with other charts that show just the opposite. The danger is that, even without realization or intent, you may find yourself presenting only the charts that support your view. Data packs the power to convince an audience of something that isn't entirely true. Statisticians and others who present data have an ethical responsibility to use this power accurately and fairly. See the Chapter 4 Commentary for more on bias and how to avoid it.

2. Diagnostic Analytics

Explanation: Descriptive analytics can surface interesting or unexpected results that raise important questions, such as "Why are few high-quality candidates accepting job offers?" or, as in the example above, "Why are high-performing reps failing to meet quotas?" Diagnostic analytics, a powerful methodology that dives deeper into the data using a variety of analytics tools, can often answer these questions very effectively.

Example: Diagnostic analytics can take many forms. In Chapters 5 and 6, Chloe effectively used the sales rep "DNA"— the quantifiable characteristics of a top rep—but where did it come from? Essentially, Chloe worked to understand how all reps behaved and how that behavior impacted sales. She first defined the *output variable,* which in this case was all reps and their level of success—bottom, middle, or top. She then assembled *input variables* for each rep: KPIs such as "leads generated" and "deal size" and other factors that affect KPIs such as "partnering with other reps" and "number of trainings." Chloe's goal was to determine which input variables impacted the output variable and to what degree.

To understand the impact of all the different combinations of input variables, she broke out the big guns: machine learning. If your eyes glaze over when you read "machine learning," fear not. In a nutshell, machine learning involves models that learn to make decisions and predictions automatically from data. Once a machine learning model has been "trained" with data, it can be thought of as a fancy black box with input and output terminals. Give the black box some input variables and it guesses what the output should be, based on data it has been trained on.

Chloe trained a black box that had multiple variables (KPIs) as inputs and sales ranking (bottom, middle, top) as output. Then she unscrewed the box's instrumentation panel and peeked inside. This enabled her to see how the black box model made use of each of the variables.

Chloe found that the model often used and reused certain variables when estimating the output, while other variables were effectively ignored. She concluded that the most frequently used variables were also the most important, and she used this information to rank the KPIs. This ranked list of KPIs, along with the amount of influence each KPI has on the output, is the sales rep DNA, which can then be used to guide training, hiring, coaching, and more.

Insight 1: There is no one correct way to do diagnostic analytics. In Chapter 5, the diagnoses were mostly descriptive analytics and some hands-on sleuthing. In Chapter 6, the diagnostic analytics—answering the question "why"—made heavy use of predictive analytics (covered next). This is true of every stage of the analytics process: there is no single "right" way to do it, and it's important to be flexible and creative as you dive into data.

Insight 2: These four stages (descriptive, diagnostic, predictive, and prescriptive) are not necessarily sequential. They're just a helpful way to divide analytics work into manageable chunks.

3. Predictive Analytics

Explanation: Once you have a good sense of what your data is telling you, it may be time to deploy predictive models. Predictive analytics approaches are about using already-collected data to train models that will attempt to generalize to other situations (in other words, to new, unseen data).

For example, the people who built your computer's spam detector trained it by feeding it millions of emails, a portion of which were spam and were identified to the model as such. After processing considerable training data emails and labels of spam versus not-spam, the model's mathematical

203

optimization routines learned to distinguish spam from legitimate email. It was then able to predict which new emails were spam with a "good enough" accuracy.

Example: In Chapter 6, Chloe discusses her approach to predicting high-producer rep attrition. In short, she'll use data from prior years to train a model to predict whether high producers will quit. This involves the same type of machine learning model that determined the sales rep DNA (see above), but it's used differently. Instead of unscrewing the black box and seeing which variables are crucial, she'll focus on using the outputs of the black box (the predictions) to figure out which reps might quit.

First, Chloe will obtain the following data:

1. Rep KPI data from 2012 to 2015

2. Rep attrition data from 2012 to 2015

3. Rep KPI data from 2016

4. Rep attrition data from 2016

Next, Chloe will train the model with data from 2012 to 2015. The model will crunch through this data and "learn" a mathematical relationship between the inputs (KPI data) and the outputs (attrition outcome). To see how accurate the model is, Chloe will feed it rep KPI data from 2016 and compare the model's predictions about which reps will quit against the actual 2016 attrition data.

If Chloe's black box model trains well, the *predicted* attrition for this second set of data will match their *actual* attrition with a "good enough" accuracy. Chloe doesn't expect an exact match, because models are never perfect, and it's simply hard to predict the future, no matter how fancy the algorithm. She just needs to know that it's going to produce reasonably reliable results.

Insight 1: Although we are presenting prescriptive analytics after discussing diagnostic analytics, both can make use of the same fundamental tools.

Insight 2: Predictive analytics isn't guaranteed to "work." When building a predictive system, your data analysts will have to try out different models, measure how well each one performs, and then decide whether to use the best model in practice. Often, the best performing model isn't good enough, in which case we can conclude that predictive analytics is not viable for this particular application given the data currently available.

4. Prescriptive Analytics

Explanation: Once you understand the deeper processes that underlie your data (descriptive analytics), have a sense of why they are happening (diagnostic analytics), and have predictions about the future (predictive analytics), the next step is to act on your knowledge. That's where prescriptive analytics comes in. It produces insights and actions intended to improve future outcomes.

Example: In Chapter 6, one of the applications of prescriptive analytics discussed is providing interventions for reps at risk of attrition. Where will these interventions come from? And who should be targeted first?

The interventions are an outgrowth of the sales rep DNA identified during the diagnostic analytics step. We can see how a given rep measures up according to the DNA and then pinpoint which important KPIs she or he is lagging in. The specific skills needed to excel at those KPIs will be the targets of our interventions, which will be determined by experts.

Say the rep is falling behind on "deal size," an important KPI. The rep's manager would then determine which enablement offerings will best help this rep increase deal size. If a significant number of reps all need to increase deal size, the L&D team may need to develop new training. We could also use predictive models to guess which reps are at risk for attrition and prioritize them for intervention.

Insight 1: Prescriptive analytics is the least established of the four types of analytics, because prescriptions are specific to each scenario and can vary widely across businesses and industries. Further, effective prescriptions are a collaborative effort between the analyst and a business expert with a deep understanding of company, employee, and customer needs. The two must work together to best leverage findings and insights from the descriptive, diagnostic, and predictive analytics stages.

Insight 2: This speaks to the importance of pairing analytics with instincts and experience. Many of the judgment calls involved in the Human Resources disciplines are too complex to replace with modern artificial intelligence or machine learning. In such cases, prescriptive analytics is about arming the experts with additional insights that will help them make better decisions than they could otherwise—and not about replicating those decisions.

HR ANALYTICS REVIEW

Introduction

In this concluding section, we want to introduce you to the many ways you can begin your analytics journey or, if you have an established program, expand and enhance your impact. The more people in Human Resources are engaged with data and analytics, the more it will be accepted in the community and within our own organizations and the more impact and success we will all (we hope) enjoy in our work and careers.

Many business books provide glowing reports about how the authors accomplished X, Y, or Z analytics initiatives in their organizations. While this can be interesting, it is often difficult to translate others' achievements into actionable programs in one's own organization. Common barriers to starting are as varied as the potential applications of analytics, but they often include: "My organization is just not ready for this level of involvement"; "My data are not clear, standardized, or readily available"; "Our legal department—or, if European-based, our data protection and privacy office—would never approve"; or, our favorite, "We just don't have the time or the skills."

We intend with this book, and this section in particular, to help demystify how you can use data analytics powerfully to transform the Human Resources functions.

Below, we have summarized key analytics concepts, outlined some typical efficiency (or "rearview mirror") metrics and more meaningful effectiveness (or impact) metrics, and offer examples of applying analytics for you to consider in your own organization. This is not an all-inclusive list, but it is intended to help you get started in the core areas:

A. Leadership Development and Succession Management
B. Learning Management
C. Performance Management
D. Talent Acquisition
E. Total Rewards

A. LEADERSHIP DEVELOPMENT AND SUCCESSION PLANNING

Summary

Leadership development can be a very murky area of human capital development, but it doesn't have to be. With a disciplined approach to measurement and analytics, professionals running these programs can gain staunch support from company executives, which is especially critical to success.

Unfortunately, at too many companies, the highest-performing person on the team is made the manager, whether or not he or she has any people management skills or even inclinations. Yet, with clearly defined criteria for promotion, including skills and behaviors, promoting new managers becomes more of a science than an art.

This carries over to succession planning. Effective organizations agree up-front what makes for successful candidates and establish a clear process to assess, identify, and develop talent who are truly ready when the opportunity arises. They also know when they can take smart risks and which essential skills or knowledge cannot be compromised. This avoids expensive and time-consuming external interviews; the wise HR professional will calculate these and other costs to make the business case for strong leadership development and succession management.

Leadership Development KPI Comparison

Efficiency Metrics	Impact Metrics
Number of leaders who have completed leadership development programs Satisfaction scores from leadership development programs	**Leadership Bench Strength** Percentage of key roles that have identified successors who are ready now Percentage of leaders who can perform multiple jobs and effectively flex between roles Percentage of leaders ready now for succession pools and succession by role **Underrepresented Leadership Candidates** Percentage of women and minorities who are ready now for next leadership roles Promotion rate of women and minorities into higher levels of leadership Identification of emerging talent for leadership pipeline

How You Might Use Analytics for Leadership Development

Objective	Method	Analytics
Build leadership bench strength	Ideal leader profiling: identify the drivers of leadership success and create profile of ideal leader and leadership KPI benchmarks	Diagnostic analysis using quantitative and qualitative inputs to identify what top leaders do differently, based on team performance, new hire ramp, retention data, customer data, upward feedback, coaching notes, engagement surveys, leadership assessments, social and digital presence
Improve leadership readiness	Data driven leadership coaching: using data-based evidence of gap areas and recommendation generation, based on ideal leader profile	Based on individual leadership readiness scoring and individual leadership scorecards of strengths and weaknesses, develop prescriptive analytics to recommend training, content, activity, education, projects, mentors, interim jobs and careers, best practices, behaviors, skills, attitudes, etc.
Fill leadership pipeline with new talent	Future leader identification	Leadership readiness scoring for identification of aspiring leaders using drivers of success analytics rather than purely based on performance rating

B. LEARNING MANAGEMENT

Summary

Too often, learning professionals are under pressure to deliver programs that are well-attended and cost-effective, not programs that drive impact. This can lead to focusing on KPIs such as percentage of courses completed and learning delivery costs, rather than examining how L&D investments drive business metrics.

The result: organizations can spend a lot of money on programs that have little if any sustainability or measurable business results. The wider HR implications include missed development opportunities for emerging or non-traditional talent and risk of losing that talent to the competition, and having to hire talent externally, usually at a much higher cost, to gain important skills.

By focusing instead on impact metrics, organizations can gain critical insights, such as which learning investments yield the greatest returns, and the extent to which learning interventions impact measurable business outcomes such as productivity, profitability, or new product introduction and adoption. Effective L&D groups can develop talent more quickly and effectively, and they can clearly show how their programs make a difference to the organization's bottom line.

Learning Management KPI Comparison

Efficiency Metrics	Impact Metrics
Course completions	**Knowledge Gained**
Cost per learner	Average before/after testing score increase
Cost per hour of learning delivered	Percent of successful certifications
Ratio of employees to training staff	Improved employee knowledgeability scores on customer feedback surveys
Kirkpatrick Level I learner evaluations ("smile sheets")	Decrease in call volume to internal employee service centers
	Behavior Change
	Adoption of new methodologies or processes
	Faster time to productivity/ competency
	Business Impact
	Revenue increase, e.g., through successful sales training
	Improvement in retention, engagement, trust, or other employee metrics
	Improvement in loyalty, retention, or other customer metrics
	Return on investment

How You Might Use Analytics for Learning Management

Objective	Method	Analytics
Prioritize learning resources according to desired business outcomes	KPI modeling	Identify KPIs most closely associated with top performers; assess how others perform on these KPIs and prioritize role-based training inventory accordingly.
Optimize learning channel investment and increase learning activity/adoption	Delivery channel and learning behavior analysis	Perform cluster analysis with data from content and LMS log files to determine which learning methods and content are most popular, assessing learning behaviors of specific groups: learning modes preferred; content accessed; frequency of access; time spent; time of day preferred; etc.
Drive consistent learning through automated, personalized learning recommendations	Prescriptive analytics	Use performance diagnostics to identify individual employees' performance issues; based on skills gaps, provide personalized learning recommendations.
Optimize just-in-time learning via online peer/social/collaborative knowledge sharing	Text analytics	Use text analysis to mine peer-driven/social/collaborative learning content (email forums, blogs, online community discussions, micro-blogging) for most popular topics and issues and consolidate/centralize by topic, thus extracting more benefit from this already-valuable information.

C. PERFORMANCE MANAGEMENT

Summary

Performance management, which for years was considered by many as a necessary evil, has emerged—remade—into a new force for positive culture and development. Too often, assessing individual and team performance to guide promotion, compensation, and other decisions was an emotional or even irrational process, done quickly and with little, if any, meaningful data. Today, however, leading-edge companies are finding data driven pathways to identifying what skills, knowledge, and abilities have proven successful and instilling them in all employees so they can up their game and provide exemplary customer and other services.

HR professionals must break out of the cycle of focusing solely on administrative mandates, such as forms being filled out correctly and review comments being legally defensible. While these must be considered, they do little to increase performance or drive business results. Instead, use analytics to unleash the opportunity to re-create a performance management system that identifies what behaviors lead to success and how to accelerate time to productivity. We present below some ideas on how do to just that.

Performance Management KPI Comparison

Efficiency Metrics	Impact Metrics
Percentage of reviews completed	**Identification of Top Performers**
	Net time between promotions
Distribution of performance classifications	Productivity or innovation metrics
	Development of Outstanding People Leaders
Percentage of identified top performers	Success profiles of top people leaders/high trust scores
	Identification and selection of underrepresented people leaders

How You Might Use Analytics for Performance Management

Objective	Method	Analytics
Better guide employees toward optimal performance	DNA of top performers	Based on the DNA of top performers, use prescriptive analytics to recommend training, content, activity, education, projects, mentors, best practices, behaviors, skills, attitude, etc., to enable employees to close gaps.
Increase leadership trust and trust-earning behaviors	Diagnostic Impact Analysis	Based on the DNA of managers with higher trust scores, identify top behaviors from 360-degree feedback, coaching conversation records, and career and performance management system records. Train other managers on these behaviors. Assess the correlation between trust scores and performance and retention metrics to help predict outcome of managers' performance based on trust scores as a leading indicator.
Help managers more effectively coach employees in a continuous learning environment	Coaching topic and recommendation analysis	Where systems exist to capture manager-employee coaching conversations, perform text analysis to identify top coaching topics by role and aggregate most frequent manager recommendations on those topics. Share with managers to help them formulate effective coaching conversations with their employees.

D. TALENT ACQUISITION

Summary

Talent Acquisition professionals are often under pressure to fill jobs quickly and at the lowest cost possible, yet by focusing on metrics that track responses to short-term stakeholder pain points—all too easy given the highly transactional nature of TA—they can lose the opportunity to measure whether they are driving positive outcomes aligned with company strategy.

In the long term, a company will be better served by KPIs that reflect the candidate experience, hiring manager experience, talent pipeline development, and, of course, whether a job candidate will be successful as an employee. These measure impact far better than efficiency metrics such as time to close or cost per hire. These metrics are not unimportant, but they can never predict candidate success, which is ultimately why Talent Acquisition exists.

In addition, more mature HR organizations are evolving their quality metrics, for example, by replacing "Time to Fill" (between req approval and candidate offer acceptance) with the more inclusive "Posting to First Day of Work," between when a job req is opened (including the approval process) and an employee's first day (encompassing delays between offer and start date and also capturing no-shows).

KPI Comparison

Efficiency Metrics	Impact Metrics
Percent of reqs open vs. closed	**New Hire Quality**
	Time to productivity, e.g., time to quota
Applicants per job posting	
Candidates shortlisted per job posting	Retention of top performers (per 9-box model)
Time to fill	Employee referral rate
Cost per hire	**Hiring Process Quality**
	Ratio of internal to external hires
	Acceptance rates of offers
	Percent of applicants meeting quality criteria: top schools, work experience at "the right" companies (A players)
	Employer Branding
	Brand awareness, via survey companies
	Glassdoor leadership ratings
	Applicant Experience
	Hiring process satisfaction rating
	Number of interviews to offer
	Percent of hiring managers trained in behavioral interviewing

How You Might Use Analytics for Talent Acquisition

Objective	Method	Analytics
Find quality candidates faster, build talent pipeline with greater accuracy, bring on board new hires more likely to succeed	Candidate profiling: more precisely identify and target quality hires for specific roles by identifying the drivers of candidate success and creating ideal candidate profiles	Diagnostic analysis using quantitative and qualitative data to identify what the employees most successful in those roles do differently; use that data to guide interview questions, candidate scoring system, etc.
Extend offers to candidates most likely to accept them	Predict likelihood to accepting an offer based on job readiness, propensity to accept, and job search activities	Predictive analytics using quantitative and qualitative data to forecast whether candidate has right skills, experience, and profile; how attractive the role should be (based on title, salary, and other factors vs. his or her current role), and candidate job search activities on LinkedIn (networking, connecting with recruiters, etc.).

E. TOTAL REWARDS

Summary

Total rewards professionals are responsible for one of the most influential tools that Human Resources has to drive new behavior or reward desired behavior. Unfortunately, too often these professionals are under pressure to control payroll and benefits costs and assure compliance without regard for the impact that these decisions have on employee engagement, innovation, and customer service.

Controlling costs and assuring compliance are important, but they alone will not have the power of a well-designed and implemented total rewards program, which can truly change behavior. A common example is sales compensation plans, which are carefully designed to drive specific sales rep activity. Other parts of the business can follow suit, for example, by rewarding customer service agents based on net promoter scores or predicating bonuses on how well leaders inspire trust.

Effective total rewards professionals advocate for programs that contribute to customer and business success, which may cost more in the short term but overall yield much higher organizational success.

Total Rewards KPI Comparison

Efficiency Metrics	Impact Metrics
Percentage of Budget Spent	**Pay for Performance**
Distribution of Budget by Performance Category	Ratio of top performers' pay to business productivity
Year Over Year Reduction in Spend	Analysis of total rewards philosophy on business outcomes
	Pay Strategy and Connection to Business Performance
	Impact of equity programs on stock price/market performance
	Variable pay correlation to business performance

How You Might Use Analytics for Total Rewards

Objective	Method	Analytics
Optimize comp spend and talent gained/retained	Compensation benchmarking	Use compensation modeling with industry-wide data to determine objective optimal compensation levels based on candidate experience, expertise, education, references, propensity to perform and stay, etc.
		Map benefits trends year on year based on employee engagement surveys, exit interviews, and hiring conversations.
		Remodel salary and benefit composition annually based on industry and internal data study.
Reduce unwanted attrition through comp optimization	Attrition intervention	Use predictive analytics to identify which employees are likely to leave because of dissatisfaction with compensation and benefits.
		Combine with predictive insights on other reasons for leaving, e.g., career growth, manager competence, employee performance, etc.
		Based on predictive inputs, use prescriptive analytics to determine optimal compensation as relevant and intervene with employee.

REFERENCES

Accenture Labs. *Retail Hyperpersonalization: Creepy or Cool?* Accenture. Last updated 2015. Accessed May 25, 2017. https://www.accenture.com/t20160728T163156__w__/ca-en/ _acnmedia/Accenture/Conversion-Assets/DotCom/Documents/Global/PDF/Dualpub_8/Accenture-Technology-Labs-Hyperpersonalization.pdf.

Anderson, Carl. *Creating a Data-Driven Organization: Practical Advice from the Trenches.* Sebastopol, CA: O'Reilly, 2015. Accessed May 16, 2017. https://books.google.com/books?id=M VpDCgAAQBAJ&pg=PA78&lpg=PA78.

Association of National Advertisers. "Marketing's Moment: Leading Disruption." Last modified October 16, 2014. Accessed May 25, 2017. http://www.ana.net/content/show/id/32226.

Bean, Randy. "Big Data and the Emergence of the Chief Data Officer." *Forbes.* Last modified August 8, 2016. Accessed May 25, 2017. https://www.forbes.com/sites/ciocentral/2016/08/08/big-data-and-the-emergence-of-the-chief-data-officer/print/.

Bersin, Josh. *Predictions for 2016: A Bold New World of Talent, Learning, Leadership, and HR Technology Ahead.* Oakland, CA: Bersin by Deloitte. Accessed May 25, 2017. https://www2 .deloitte.com/content/dam/Deloitte/at/Documents/human-capital/bersin-predictions-2016.pdf.

Bersin, Josh, Karen O'Leonard, and Wendy Wang-Audia. *High-Impact Talent Analytics: Building a World-Class HR Measurement and*

Analytics Function. Oakland, CA: Bersin & Associates, October 2013. Accessed May 25, 2017. http://www.bersin.com/Lib/Rs/ ShowDocument.aspx?docid=16909.

Birnbaum, Phil. "A Guide to Sabermetric Research." Phoenix, AZ: Society for American Baseball Research. Accessed May 25, 2017. http://sabr.org/sabermetrics/single-page.

Brajkovich, Leo F., and Victor J. Reyes. "Using Workforce Analytics to Deliver Your Business Strategy." HR.com. Last modified November 18, 2015. Accessed May 25, 2017. https://www.hr.com/en?t=/ network/event/attachment.supply&fileID=1447773089804.

CEB Global. "Rethinking the Workforce Survey." Arlington, VA: CEB Global, 2015. Accessed May 25, 2017. https://www.cebglobal .com/content/dam/cebglobal/us/EN/talent-management/ workforce-surveys/pdfs/ws-fwe-rethinkingtheworkforcesurvey -clearadvantage-wp.pdf.

Christensen, Clayton N. *The Innovator's Dilemma: The Revolutionary Book That Will Change the Way You Do Business*. New York: HarperBusiness, 1997/2011.

Collins, Jim, and Jerry I. Porras. *Built to Last: Successful Habits of Visionary Companies*. New York: HarperBusiness, 1994.

Collins, Laurence, Dave Fineman, and Akio Tsuchida. "People Analytics: Recalculating the Route." In *Global Human Capital Trends 2017*, ed. Bill Pelster and Jeff Schwartz, 97–105. Westlake, TX: Deloitte University Press. Accessed May 25, 2017. https://dupress.deloitte.com/content/dam/dup-us-en/articles/ HCTrends_2017/DUP_Global-Human-capital-trends_2017.pdf.

Court, David. "Getting Big Impact from Big Data." *McKinsey Quarterly*, January 2015. Accessed May 25, 2017. http://www.mckinsey .com/business-functions/digital-mckinsey/our-insights/getting -big-impact-from-big-data.

Davenport, Thomas H., and D.J. Patil. "Data Scientist: The Sexiest Job of the 21st Century." *Harvard Business Review*, October 2012.

Accessed May 25, 2017. http://hbr.org/2012/10/data-scientist -the-sexiest-job-of-the-21st-century/ar/pr.

Dearborn, Jenny. *Data Driven: How Performance Analytics Delivers Extraordinary Results*. Hoboken, NJ: John Wiley & Sons, 2015.

Frey, Carl Benedict, and Michael A. Osborne. *"The Future of Employment: How Susceptible Are Jobs to Computerisation?"* Unpublished paper, Oxford Martin School, University of Oxford, September 17, 2013. Accessed May 25, 2017. http://www .oxfordmartin.ox.ac.uk/downloads/academic/The_Future_of_ Employment.pdf.

Harter, Jim, and Annamarie Mann. "The Right Culture: Not About Employee Happiness," *Gallup Business Journal*. Last modified April 12, 2017. Accessed May 25, 2017. http://www.gallup.com/ businessjournal/208487/right-culture-not-employee-happiness .aspx?version=print.

Harvard Business Review Analytics Services. *HR Joins the Analytics Revolution*. Brighton, MA: Harvard Business Publishing, July 2014. Accessed May 25, 2017. https://hbr.org/resources/pdfs/ comm/visier/18765_HBR_Visier_Report_July2014.pdf.

Henke, Nicholas, Jacques Bughin, Michael Chui, James Manyika, Tamim Saleh, Bill Wiseman, and Guru Sethupathy. *The Age of Analytics: Competing in a Data-Driven World*. New York: McKinsey Global Institute, December 2016. Accessed May 25, 2017. http:// www.mckinsey.com/business-functions/mckinsey-analytics/our -insights/the-age-of-analytics-competing-in-a-data-driven-world.

Heskett, James L., Thomas O. Jones, Gary W. Loveman, W. Earl Sasser, Jr., and Leonard A. Schlesinger. "Putting the Service-Profit Chain to Work," *Harvard Business Review*, 1994, republished July/August 2008. Accessed May 10, 2017. https://hbr .org/2008/07/putting-the-service-profit-chain-to-work.

Kantrowitz, Tracy M. *Global Assessment Trends 2014*. London: CEB Global, 2015. Accessed May 25, 2017. https://www.cebglobal

.com/content/dam/cebglobal/us/EN/regions/uk/tm/pdfs/
Report/gatr-2014.pdf.

Kowske, Brenda. *The Employee Engagement Primer*. Oakland, CA:
Bersin & Associates, January 2012. Accessed May 25, 2017. http://
www.bersin.com/Lib/Rs/ShowDocument.aspx?docid=15197.

Lewis, Michael. *Moneyball: The Art of Winning an Unfair Game*.
New York: W.W. Norton, 2003.

Lohr, Steve. "How Big Data Became So Big." *New York Times*,
August 12, 2012. Accessed May 25, 2017. http://www.nytimes
.com/2012/08/12/business/how-big-data-became-so-big
-unboxed.html?_r=0&pagewanted=print.

ManpowerGroup, *2016/2017 Talent Shortage Survey*. Milwaukee,
WI: ManpowerGroup, 2017. Accessed May 25, 2017. http://
www.manpowergroup.us/campaigns/talent-shortage/assets/
pdf/2016-Talent-Shortage-Infographic.pdf.

Manyika, James, Michael Chui, Mehdi Miremadi, Jacques Bughin,
Katy George, Paul Willmott, and Martin Dewhurst. "Harnessing
Automation for a Future That Works." *McKinsey Global Institute Report*, January 2017. Accessed May 25, 2017. http://www
.mckinsey.com/global-themes/digital-disruption/harnessing
-automation-for-a-future-that-works.

Marr, Bernard. "The Complete Beginner's Guide to Big Data in
2017." *Forbes*. Last modified March 14, 2017. Accessed May 25,
2017. https://www.forbes.com/sites/bernardmarr/2017/03/14/
the-complete-beginners-guide-to-big-data-in-2017/print/.

Mauboussin, Michael J. "The True Measures of Success." *Harvard
Business Review*, October 2012. Accessed May 25, 2017. https://
hbr.org/2012/10/the-true-measures-of-success.

McAfee, Andrew, and Erik Brynjolfsson. "Big Data: The Management Revolution." *Harvard Business Review*, October 2012.
Accessed May 25, 2017. https://hbr.org/2012/10/big-data-the
-management-revolution

Miller, Steven, and Debbie Hughes. *The Quant Crunch: How the Demand for Data Science Skills Is Disrupting the Job Market.* Boston, MA: Burning Glass Technologies, 2017. Accessed May 16, 2017. https://www-01.ibm.com/common/ssi/cgi-bin/ssialias?htmlfid=IML14576USEN.

Oehler, Ken. *2015 Trends in Global Employee Engagement.* London: Aon plc, 2015. Accessed May 25, 2017. http://www.aon.com/attachments/human-capital-consulting/2015-Trends-in-Global-Employee-Engagement-Report.pdf.

Oxford Economics. *Workforce 2020: The Looming Talent Crisis.* New York: Oxford Economics, September 2014. Accessed May 25, 2017. https://www.oxfordeconomics.com/publication/open/250945.

Pelster, Bill, and Jeff Schwartz (eds.). *Global Human Capital Trends 2017.* Westlake, TX: Deloitte UP, March 2017. Accessed May 25, 2017. https://dupress.deloitte.com/dup-us-en/focus/human-capital-trends.html.

Porter, Michael E. *Competitive Advantage: Creating and Sustaining Superior Performance.* New York: The Free Press, 1985.

PwC. *Global CEO Survey: The Talent Challenge.* London: PwC, 2014. Accessed May 25, 2017. http://www.pwc.com/gx/en/hr-management-services/publications/assets/ceosurvey-talent-challenge.pdf.

Reid, Claire, Richard Petley, Julie McLean, Kieran Jones, and Peter Ruck. *Seizing the Information Advantage: How Organizations Can Unlock Value and Insight from the Information They Hold.* London: PwC/Iron Mountain, September 2015. Accessed May 25, 2017. http://www.ironmountain.com/Knowledge-Center/Reference-Library/View-by-Document-Type/White-Papers-Briefs/S/Seizing-The-Information-Advantage-Executive-Summary.aspx.

Sardana, Sanjeev, and Sandeep Sardana. "Big Data: It's Not a Buzzword; It's a Movement." *Forbes.* Last modified November 20,

2013. Accessed May 25, 2017. https://www.forbes.com/sites/sanjeevsardana/2013/11/20/bigdata/.

Schwab, Klaus. *The Fourth Industrial Revolution*. New York: Crown Business, 2017.

Stanton, Jeffrey. *An Introduction to Data Science*. Syracuse, NY: n.p., 2013. Accessed May 25, 2017. https://archive.org/details/DataScienceBookV3.

University of Exeter. "The Change Curve." Accessed May 25, 2017. http://www.exeter.ac.uk/media/universityofexeter/humanresources/documents/learningdevelopment/the_change_curve.pdf.

van der Muelen, Rob. "2017: The Year That Data and Analytics Go Mainstream." Stamford, CT: Gartner, Inc. Last modified January 24, 2017. Accessed May 25, 2017. http://www.gartner.com/smarterwithgartner/2017-the-year-that-data-and-analytics-go-mainstream/.

Volini, Erica, Pascal Occean, Michael Stephan, and Brett Walsh. "Digital HR: Platforms, People, Work." In *Global Human Capital Trends 2017*, ed. Bill Pelster and Jeff Schwartz, 87–94. Westlake, TX: Deloitte University Press. Accessed May 25, 2017. https://dupress.deloitte.com/content/dam/dup-us-en/articles/HCTrends_2017/DUP_Global-Human-capital-trends_2017.pdf.

Waddell, Kaveh. "The Algorithms That Tell Bosses How Employees Are Feeling." *The Atlantic*, September 29, 2016. Accessed May 25, 2017. https://www.theatlantic.com/technology/archive/2016/09/the-algorithms-that-tell-bosses-how-employees-feel/502064/.

ABOUT THE AUTHORS

Jenny Dearborn is the author of the 2015 business best-seller *Data Driven: How Performance Analytics Delivers Extraordinary Sales Results*. She is recognized as one of the fifty most powerful women in technology and is an industry thought leader and authority on applying data and analytics to workforce development and human capital transformation. At SAP, the world's largest business software company, she is responsible for learning, development, talent management, leadership, succession management, and organization development for the approximately 90,000 SAP employees worldwide.

Dearborn is a frequent contributor to the mainstream business press and is an internationally sought-after keynote speaker. She is a graduate of American River College, the University of California–Berkeley, Stanford University, and San Jose State University and sits on several boards of directors.

She lives with her family in Palo Alto, California, and in Montecito, California. She can be reached at

@DearbornJenny

https://www.linkedin.com/in/jdearborn/

David Swanson has more than thirty years of human resource management experience. He was most recently executive vice president of human resources for SAP Success-Factors, partnering with the company's sales organization to showcase how SAP is using SAP HR. Prior to that, he served as chief human resources officer for SAP North America and global head of HR for SAP's products and innovation organization, where he delivered the people strategy to drive business performance. In addition, he has held executive human resources positions at a number of technology companies, supporting global development, marketing, sales and service organizations.

Swanson is a keynote speaker and panelist on the future of HR, focusing on how HR can impact business through analytics and big data. He actively supports the human resources community as a board member of the Bay Area Human Resources Executive Council (BAHREC) and a regular presenter and facilitator with the Society for Human Resource Management (SHRM) and the Northern California Human Resources Association (NCHRA). Swanson is on the innovation advisory board of the Hult International Business School and an adjunct lecturer with the University of California, Santa Cruz Extension.

He lives with his family in the Santa Cruz, California, mountains. He can be reached at
@DavidSwansonHR
https://www.linkedin.com/in/davidswansonhr

INDEX

Fictional companies and employees are listed in italics and page references followed by *fig* indicate an illustrated figure.

at *Trajectory,* 58; talent
acquisition, 217–218;
variable as another term
for, 70, 202. *See also* Talent
acquisition KPIs
Kübler-Ross Change Curve,
142–143

L

Leadership: as key to building
data analytics capability,
193; leadership development
and succession planning for,
208–210; underrepresented
candidates for, 209. *See also*
Exalted senior leadership
Leadership development:
data analytics applied
to succession planning
and, 208–209, 210; KPI
comparison of efficiency
and impact metrics, 209;
underrepresented candidates
for, 209
Learning & Development: asked
to create product sheets
on acquired products, 141;
Bobby's continued rejection
of, 61, 99, 102; leadership
development/succession
planning by, 208–210;
learning management by,
211–213; organizations
that use completions as
a success metric, 43–44;
predictive analytics on
at-risk producers failing to
complete, 155, 158; special
coaching and training
through, 186, 188, 216; what

collected data indicates
about attrition and, 98–102.
See also Enablement
Learning management:
comparison of KPIs for, 212;
data analytics applied to,
211, 213
Lee, Martha (VP of HR Centers
of Excellence): applying
predictive analytics
to improve sales rep
performance, 148, 153,
157, 160, 166, 168; on
demoralized employees,
8; on findings of initial
attribution data, 87, 94, 98,
99, 102; on findings of the
attribution data, 117, 122,
127, 130, 141; on improving
Exalted's hiring process, 32,
33–34, 38–39; on the sales
attribution problem, 12, 13,
17–18; sales rep attrition
data analytics contributions
by, 51, 52, 54, 56, 61, 63, 70;
strategic planning meeting
with, 6–16, 17–18, 22*fig*
Lewis, Michael, 109
LinkedIn, 64
Long, Marcus (VP of HR
Business Partners): applying
predicative analytics to
sales rep performance, 148,
151, 152–153, 160, 161; on
findings of attrition data,
117, 118, 122, 123, 126, 127,
130, 132, 134, 135–137, 138;
on findings of initial attrition
data, 84, 87, 90, 94, 102,
104; on improving *Exalted's*
hiring process, 31–32, 36–37,

Products: Bobby's complaints about *Exalted's* new, 131; challenges of changing *Exalted's,* 127–128; data on *Exalted's* low revenue from new, 7, 178; data showing how engagement increases revenue from new, 179–180; failure to use change management supporting new, 128, 140–141; Martha's Learning & Development product sheets on new, 141; as sales reps attrition ecosystem factor, 126–127, 149, 150, 184–188

PwC data analytics survey, 20

Q

Quota attainment: data on unattainable top producer, 97, 200; data on unrealistic *Exalted,* 94–98; as key driver of sales reps attribution ecosystem, 94, 112, 149, 150, 184–188; predictive analytics on at-risk high producers and their, 155

R

Retention risk analysis, 152–154

Retention. *See* Sales reps retention

Revenue: data on *Exalted's* low, 7, 178; data showing how engagement drives up, 179–180; parallel decline of sales engagement, retention, and, 120, 143–144

Rodriquez, Anne (chief marketing officer): introduction to the, 5; responding to data access request, 84–87, 104, 105; responding to findings of attrition data, 133–135, 136, 141–142; support of Pam's presentation to the board by, 176, 182, 186, 191; on *Thomas Ashcroft's* strategies as mentor to her, 85–86, 104, 133, 134, 135

S

Sales rep attrition: collecting data on, 59–71; correlation versus causation of, 92, 109–110; employer brand factor, 64–65, 88, 117; high rate of past, 7, 178; top producer versus performer, 56, 90, 94–98, 155–157, 200, 215; total rewards data analytics applied to decrease, 220–222. *See also* Sales rep attrition ecosystem; Stem rep attrition plan

Sales rep attrition data: collecting and team discussion of the, 84–108; connecting the dots of the, 107–108; correlation versus causation issue of, 92, 109–110; determining which variables most impact *Trajectory,* 58; diagnosing the "why" of, 112–144; evidence on value of enabling development, 98–103; *Exalted's* high